SHOULD THE PATIENT KNOW THE TRUTH?

SHOULD THE PATIENT KNOW THE TRUTH?

A RESPONSE

of physicians, nurses, clergymen, and lawyers

Edited by
Samuel Standard, M.D.
and
Helmuth Nathan, M.D.

Springer Science+Business Media, LLC 1955

Originally Published By Springer Publishing Company, Inc. in 1955
Softcover reprint of the hardcover 1st edition 1955

ISBN 978-3-662-39421-2 ISBN 978-3-662-40485-0 (eBook)
DOI 10.1007/978-3-662-40485-0

Library of Congress Catalog Card Number: 55-8777

EDITORS

SAMUEL STANDARD, M.D.

Associate Professor of Clinical Surgery, New York University College of Medicine; Attending Surgeon, Bellevue Hospital and University Hospital; Director of Surgery, Sydenham Hospital, New York

HELMUTH NATHAN, M.D.

Assistant Professor of Surgery, Albert Einstein College of Medicine, New York; Visiting Surgeon, Bronx Municipal Medical Center

CONTRIBUTORS

SISTER BERNADETTE ARMIGER, R.N., M.S.

Coordinator Medical and Surgical Nursing, Catherine Labouré School of Nursing, Dorchester, Massachusetts

RUTH FRANK BAER, R.N., M.N.

Formerly Instructor Pediatric Nursing, University of Illinois School of Nursing

E. M. BLUESTONE, M.D.

Consultant, Montefiore Hospital, New York

J. V. LANGMEAD CASSERLEY, D. Litt.

Mary Crooke Hoffman Professor of Dogmatic Theology, The General Theological Seminary, New York

HENRY W. CAVE, M.D.

Consultant in Surgery, The Roosevelt Hospital, New York

LEO M. DAVIDOFF, M.D.
Professor and Chairman, Department of Surgery, Albert Einstein College of Medicine, and Director of Surgery, Bronx Municipal Hospital Center; Chief of Neurosurgery, The Mount Sinai Hospital, New York

BRUNO FURST, LL.D.
Instructor, Adult Education Division, Brooklyn College

MARTIN G. GOLDNER, M.D.
Clinical Associate Professor of Medicine, State Univerversity of New York College of Medicine at New York City; Director of Medicine, Jewish Chronic Disease Hospital, Brooklyn

JOHN A. GOODWINE, S.T.L., J.C.D.
Professor of Moral Theology, St. Joseph's Seminary, Dunwoodie, Yonkers, New York

ALAN F. GUTTMACHER, M.D.
Director, Department of Obstetrics and Gynecology, The Mount Sinai Hospital, New York

RICHARD M. HONIG, Dr. jur.
Professor Emeritus, University of Göttingen

ELOISE R. LEWIS, R.N., M.S.
Associate Professor, Surgical Nursing, The University of North Carolina, Chapel Hill, North Carolina

WILLIAM F. MARTIN
Attorney, New York

BERNARD C. MEYER, M.D.
Associate Attending Psychiatrist, The Mount Sinai Hospital, New York

LOUIS I. NEWMAN, Ph.D., D.D.
Rabbi of Congregation Rodeph Sholom, New York

SAMUEL Z. ORGEL, M.D.
Instructor and Preceptor to Residents in Psychiatry, and Attending Psychiatrist, Hillside Hospital, Glen Oaks, New York

ISIDORE SNAPPER, M.D.
Director of Medicine and Medical Education, Beth-El Hospital, Brooklyn

ESTHER K. SUMP, R.N., M.S.
Associate Professor, Medical Nursing, The University of North Carolina, Chapel Hill, North Carolina

OWEN H. WANGENSTEEN, M.D., Ph.D.
Professor of Surgery; Head Department of Surgery, University of Minnesota, The Medical School

M. OLGA WEISS, R.N., M.Litt.
Associate Editor, Nursing Outlook, New York

PAUL D. WHITE, M.D.
Executive Director, National Advisory Heart Council; Consultant in Medicine, Massachusetts General Hospital, Boston

EDITH S. WOLF, R.N., A.M.
Associate Director, Nursing Education, Memorial Center for Cancer and Allied Diseases, New York

ILSE S. WOLFF, R.N., M.A.
Mental Health Nursing Consultant, Connecticut State Department of Health, Hartford

PREFACE

The question "Should the patient know the truth?" is asked often and by many people though not always in these words. As we are asking it and have made it the title of the book, the question centers around the patient, which is what finally counts. The problem of truth is discussed within the realm of medicine and, more specifically, therapy. Will it help or hurt a particular patient to know the truth about his disease? Moral and ethical issues, philosophic thought and religious beliefs, even legal considerations may enter into finding the answer, but it always remains a question of caring for a *sick* person.

The book is written by members of the professions who must find the answer and the best way to handle the giving or withholding of information to the patient. The authors are surgeons, internists, psychiatrists; nurses active in various fields; clergymen representing different faiths; and experts in law. Several of them had discussed the subject at a meeting at the New York Academy of Medicine, when the idea of a more inclusive book began to form. The circle of discussants, therefore, was widened, and we believe it is fortunate, indeed, for the scope and balance of the discussion that nurses have joined the original all-male forum.

Many, many patients are silent contributors to the

ideas and conclusions gathered in this book, and the opinions of some patients are stated directly. There is one other very large group of people concerned with the problem of the book, the families of the patient. The often difficult part they play is discussed in its importance to the patient, to themselves, and to nurses and doctors.

We wish to thank all contributors, new and old, named and silent, for their response to the question "Should the patient know the truth?" The book is small, but it seems to us that its value and impact is bigger even than the sum of its answers.

New York
March, 1955

SAMUEL STANDARD, M.D.
HELMUTH NATHAN, M.D.

SHOULD THE PATIENT KNOW THE TRUTH?

CONTENTS

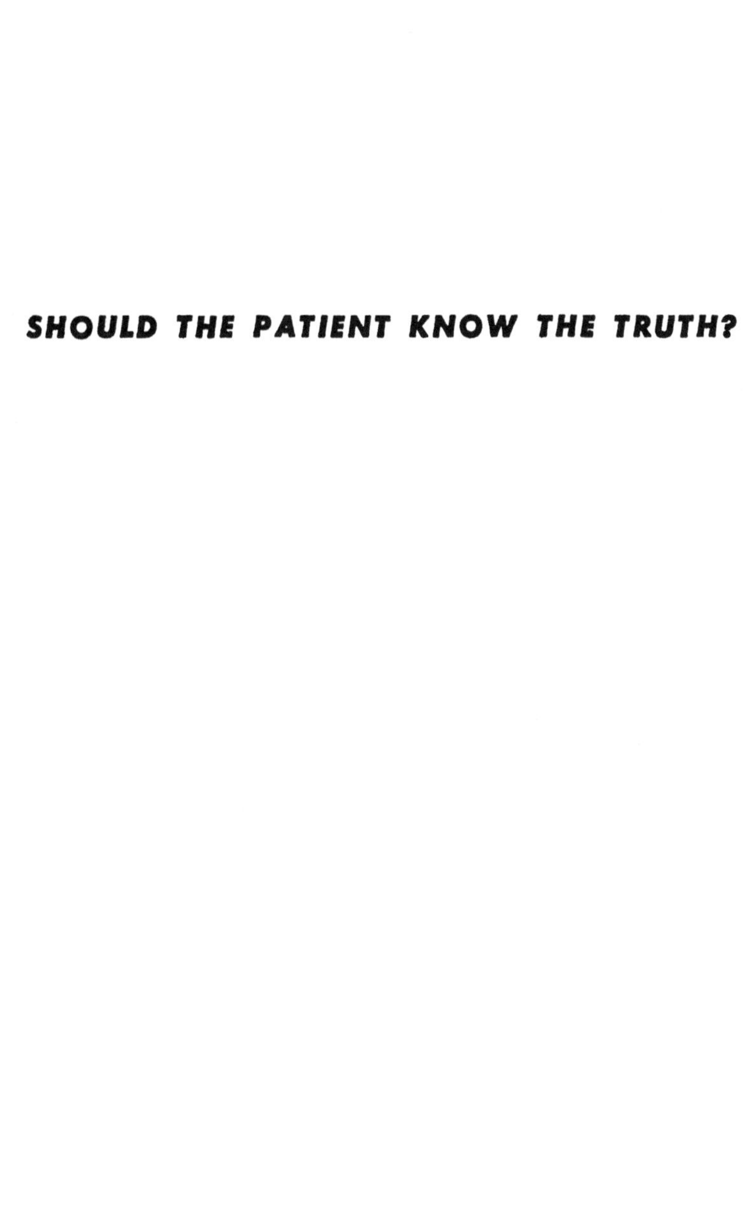

SHOULD THE PATIENT KNOW THE TRUTH?

THE SCOPE OF THE PROBLEM

Truth, An Instrument in Therapy

By Samuel Standard, M.D.

Justice Cardozo once said that no law is enacted until it has already been broken. Obviously, in a society where nobody stole there would be no need for a law to prohibit stealing. In the same talk he defined a law as something that 90 percent of the people would respect and obey. It is not something that a legislative body passes and a police officer enforces. It is something that the people as a whole, or almost as a whole, are willing to accept.

The question "Should the patient know the truth?" implies, that some patients are not told the truth, and, therefore, a discussion such as this comes up. But let's first take the points of agreement. It is generally agreed that the doctor wants the patient to do as well as present knowledge of therapy permits. It is agreed that the patient should be given the therapy he needs for his recovery and be denied anything that hinders his recovery. It is agreed that the decisions on therapy should arise from the doctor's knowledge of the disease and of the man who houses the disease. It is further agreed that the doctor is ethically bound to come to his decisions in the treatment of the patient on medical grounds. He may not let his medical judgment be warped by extra-medical considerations; if course A is the proper treatment of the patient, the doctor has no right to choose course B because it would be financially more rewarding to him, or course C because it would be a lesser burden on his conscience.

The question "Should the Patient Know the Truth?" is easily answered. Truth becomes an instrument in therapy. The answer is yes, if the knowledge of the truth will improve the patient's prospects of recovery. The answer must be no, if the knowledge of the truth will diminish his prospects of recovery.

Whether the patient will be helped or hindered by any kind of therapy, however, is not always an easy and not always a clear-cut decision. Often it is difficult to know whether a patient should be given one anti-biotic or another; whether he needs oxygen at the moment, or not; whether in his chemical imbalance it is sodium or pottassium or both that require replenishment. Medicine is not an exact science, and these decisions are rarely in the realm of 100 percent good and nothing bad. In making a decision the ratio of good to bad may be 80 to 20, or 70 to 30, and so on, and at times it gets uncomfortably close to a fifty-fifty chance. Usually one comes to a decision on grounds that are predominantly predictable. Occassionally one is wrong. It is just as important and just as trying for the physician to decide whether or not his patient needs truth and should get it or be spared knowing it.

One often hears of small untruths, that smooth the way of living with one's fellow man, as white lies, as against the black lie that is aimed to injure the person to whom it is told. It might not be out of place to say that truth, too, may be classified as white or black. As white lies are accepted within the realm of normal, honest people's behavior patterns, black truths perhaps should be banned from that realm.

It might be well to review briefly the attitudes of the

medical profession towards the patient generally. There are physicians who hold that the patient should be told very little of his disease or of his outlook, so that we might ask, "Should the patient be told anything?" These physicians literally do not speak to their patients, because of lack of time, lack of patience to find elementary explanations, or lack of respect for the patient's capacity to understand. They assume a papa-knows-best attitude and expect the patient to accept such paternalism without questioning, and many patients do accept it. At present, with the easy dissemination of knowledge through the press, radio, and television, the population as a whole is learning a great deal about medicine, and patients often demand explanations. They are entitled to them.

Medicine in the past was allied with magic and religion. The medicine man in savage countries who healed with incantations had no need to tell the patient the source of his knowledge or explain the power of his ministrations. The priest, the most literate and the most educated man of the community in olden days, knew very little about medicine; he healed with blessings and gave no explanations. These qualities hang over, and even today some physicians feel that so long as they know, or think they know, what the patient's illness is and what therapy he requires for his recovery there is no reason for the patient to question, nor for the doctor to explain.

Probably the main reason why people differ in their answers to the question, "Should the patient know the truth?" is that truth, as truth, is an accepted ethical concept in human behavior, and lying is considered something less than admirable. Among religious people lying gets to be a sin of such great importance that it may jeopardize the immortal soul in the hereafter. Before deciding that lying is done only by evil people, it might be well to think back to Justice Cardozo's definition of the law. If 90 percent of the people do not respect or obey a law, it is not a law. The question then is whether nine out of ten people respect and obey the moral or ethical law of truth.

Lying is a much more widespread habit than is generally conceded. Most people lie in small or large ways, and if lying per se is a sinful deed, then, all of us have sinned. How often have we refused an invitation by saying we had another engagement when we really had none? How often have we thanked the hostess for the wonderful time we spent at her house when actually we had been bored throughout the evening? "Isn't she beautiful?" asks the adoring mother of you as she leans over her first-born child in the crib. You look at the bundle of plainness and say, with a properly awe-struck voice, "*That's* a baby," and the mother's face lights up in gratitude at your recognition of her hopes. You achieved your deception without having to say, "That's a beautiful baby." Why should we tell this mother the truth? Laurence Sterne, in another context, has said, "Whip me such moralists." Are these white lies versus black ones? Shade them as you will.

There are lies that are not spoken or written. By a gesture, by a facial expression, by an inflection one makes a statement that is true but carries the germ of deception in it. An evasion of the truth is a lie. A mother who will not stop her child from wanting his eighth cookie by telling him the truth, that it is bad for him, will succeed in cheating him out of that cookie by giving him a toy or by drawing his attention to music. She achieves her object through deception knowing that explanation and logic are bound to fail. We don't change completely when we grow up. Mark Twain once said that he wrote books for children of all ages. Adult patients sometimes have to be treated like children. When the doctor deflects the patient's course of questioning he acts exactly like the mother of the small boy with the cookies. Or take the surgeon who comes into a patient's room the day after an operation for cancer that could not be resected. The surgeon arrives with a bouncy spring in his walk, a smile on his face, and a "You look well this morning" on his lips. He does not tell a lie, but his intent is to deceive, and he will succeed, since the patient would not admit the thought that his doctor could be so happy and gay if he, the patient, were sick unto death. This surgeon has lied, of course, and the instrument used for the deception makes no difference.

It must be accepted that the doctor may err in his decision about what he will tell the patient. The following case is an example: A young woman with infectious hepatitis was cared for by a competent physician who decided that it would be best not to tell her that this disease may last as long as twenty weeks. He told her it would take five or six weeks; if necessary, he would later on prolong the period until she recovered. The patient was doing well, but her disease was one that was going to last the full twenty weeks. When the eighth week was up and the patient was still not back to her former strength, she became panic-stricken and felt sure she was suffering from an incurable disease which would kill her. The physician had made one mistake. He should have told his patient the moment he saw her that she might be sick for four months or more. He had been wrong, primarily, in sizing up his patient and this had led him to color the information he gave her. When things seemed hopeless to the patient, she was told about the usual course of the disease and, fortunately, was able to accept the fact and go on to recovery without further mental suffering.

Most physicians would agree that the easiest way for themselves is to tell the truth and the whole truth. Then, the physician need no longer dissimulate before his patient nor worry every time he sees him to remember what untruths he told before. In practically all cases the patient is told the truth. But think of a woman who had a breast removed that already showed axillary metastasis. The doctor may tell her simply that she had a cancer of the breast with axillary metastasis and that her chance of surviving five years is one in three. He has told the truth. His responsibility is over. His conscience is clear. In a case like this, for the interest of the patient, it may be better to bend the truth, to tell only part of the truth, to skim the truth tangentially, so to speak, or perhaps tell an outright lie. Any doctor who has taken care of sick people has recognized these situations. What has he done? He has lied. There are circumstances, there are people, there are times that make fixed rules of conduct, moral, ethical or even religious, a rather debatable quality. When such a moment comes, those very concepts should guide a man to break them for the greater good—to save the patient first and paste together the fragments of one's shattered conscience at a later date. These are the risks we must all take with our soul. Robert Frost [1] in his short poem "Bravado" says it most simply:

> Have I not walked without an upward look
> Of caution under stars that very well
> Might not have missed me when they shot and fell?
> It was a risk I had to take, and took.

There are some surgeons and physicians who believe that the patient should always be told the entire truth. But do they always tell it? They may tell a woman that she had a cancer of the breast, but what the woman wants to know is whether she will live with it. They will not tell her that she has one chance in three to live if her disease had spread to the armpits; or that she has one chance out of ten to have cancer in the other breast. When a man has lost his leg because of arteriosclerotic endarteritis, he has this disease throughout his body, and in many cases he may come to amputation of the other leg. Will the doctor tell this man that he has lost this leg today and will lose the other one in two years?

What is it that may make telling the whole truth so brutal? There are few people who will continue to fight, who will continue to be part of life once they know that they are lost. A shipwrecked sailor who survives the ordeal of drifting on a limitless ocean for days or weeks owes much of his ability to continue the struggle each day to his abiding faith that rescue will come. The physician must beware not to break this will to live in his patients. There are few who will continue to live bravely and freely when they know that their end is near. If this quality of strength is found in a patient, the physician will tell him the truth. Yet, for the very few that possess this strength one may not create despair and hopelessness in the many not so constituted.

Whatever the decision reached, the doctor, the nurse, the social worker, and the patient's relatives must all understand what it is that the patient is to be told. Everyone must be briefed. The doctor may step into the room, make his Delphic statement, and depart before the patient can formulate the questions that he wants answered. The presence of interns and residents at the visit may further hamper the patient's free expression to the doctor.

The most difficult part revolves around the nurse who is chained to the patient's bedside for a full day and must carry out what in the opinion of the doctor is the best way to handle the giving or withholding of information to the patient. She cannot turn him away with a quip. She cannot leave the room to seek an answer. She must play it by ear. She must be intellectually dexterous and have the reflexed response of a trained athlete on a playing field in order to give the sound and spirit of authenticity. A delayed, contrived answer may bare the truth which she is trying to conceal.

When the patient arrives home, the family's situation becomes difficult because of the constant exposure to the patient. If it is the doctor's decision not to tell the patient the truth, then it is best to take into *this* confidence as few of the family as is consistent with responsibility for the patient. This should be done not so much to spare the other members of the family the anguish of the truth but to limit the possibility of the truth filtering back to the patient. A husband and wife usually know each other so well that the slightest digression from reality is recognized. A son may be willing to take the responsibility for the truth and not tell his parents of the other's illness. The spouse then will act hopefully and so the patient, too, will feel that his future is assured.

When, however, the patient is nearing the end, it is often better for the family to come close to him and not to continue saying that this is just a passing thing that will be over. The patient's realization that his family understands his plight will then be found of comfort. By such understanding the family, in effect, says to him: "Yes, we are in difficulty but we have been in difficulty before, and we will see our way through this one. You are not alone, the family is with you, the whole medical profession is with you, and everything that can be done is being done to make you better."

It is important that we remember the changing status of a dying man. When a patient is nearing death, the dying process is physiologically a universal one. Brain, heart, kidney—all parts die a little at a time until all life ends. The patient's sensibilities wane but each step towards his end is short and remains unnoticed in the course of a gradually diminishing life activity. One sometimes feels that a patient is pretending that things are better than they are. He probably is not. He is living a life of his kind for that moment. This is seen plainly in a chronic disease associated with slowly progressive anemia. The patient when reaching a physician complains of tiredness, weakness, easy fatigue, breathlessness, loss of mental concentrating powers, apathy to former interests. If all of these ills had come upon the patient suddenly, he would have been overwhelmed by the impact. Yet each quantity of disability, added to a growing load, was barely perceived by the patient. Only when friends point out the dramatic transformation from the person they know does it dawn upon him that something dreadful has taken place without his being aware of it. This man is not pretending. His faculties for recognition of change have deteriorated from the same cause that produced the change itself. It is unlikely that the thought of his impending death obsesses the patient. He wants to be relieved of the difficulties imposed upon him by his disease. It does not enter his thinking that pain, cough, sleeplessness, or breathlessness may be the early harbingers of inevitable death. To inform him that they are the forerunners of death can be no comfort to him and can only add fear to his suffering, "the dread of something after death, the undiscovered country from whose bourn no traveller returns."

There is one time when most physicians believe the truth should be told and should be told baldly without euphemisms. When a patient with known malignant disease, that has a good chance for cure, is not aware of the danger of his disease and refuses to be operated upon, every effort should first be made to persuade him to agree to the operation. If these efforts fail, he must be told in terms that he understands, that he has cancer, that cancer ultimately kills, and that subjecting himself to surgery, though it may not succeed, gives him the only opportunity for recovery that we know at present.

Untruth requires preparation if it is to carry validity with the patient. A woman with a tumor of the breast should not be told, if one wants to withhold the truth about cancer from her, that the breast will be left on if the frozen section is benign; and that the breast will be removed if the section is malignant. When the patient awakes without the breast, she knows she has had a cancer. The better way to handle this is to avoid an either-or alternative and to tell the patient that there is a middle ground —tumors that are now benign but of a microscopic appearance which indicates that they will turn malignant in the vast majority of cases. These are the cases, we point out, in which surgery gets good results, the cases that are gotten early in which we take the breast off as a prophylactic measure so that the patient will not continue to live with the sword of Damocles over her head. When the patient awakes without the breast, she is told that hers was this third kind of lesion. Patients generally accept this with gratitude and feel they have escaped having had cancer.

The reasons why some surgeons do not tell these patients they had cancer are fairly simple. The patient may be cured, since cancer of the breast, particularly, gives almost a 70 percent cure when there is no axillary involvement. If they are cured, they live their life freely and without fear that the disease may descend upon them again. If they are among those that will not be cured, they live two or three or four years with that same freedom. When metastatic disease occurs, they can be told that it is some other illness, whereas if they know they had cancer they would know this means the end. Some women with such breast cancers survive many years. They receive therapy following each appearance of a metastatic deposit, and not knowing that their disease will ultimately be fatal live their final years with hope.

Preparation for a patient who will be left with a colostomy requires the same kind of forethought. A way to handle the problem is to inform the patient before the operation that he may be left with an abdominal anus, that this may be a temporary opening (the impression is left that it is usual to keep the colostomy open for six months), and that at the end of such period the decision will be made as to whether normal bowel continuity can be restored. When the patient is in the early days of his colostomy, which are rugged days for him, he bears them better with the thought that this is a temporary expedient. He is taught how to use the irrigating apparatus, he finds that he can go out into society with safety, and as the end of the six months approaches he becomes less and less insistent in his questions about restoration. Most patients, however, look forward to the end of this period with great anticipation. The surgeon will then imply that perhaps there are more cases that cannot be closed than the patient might have thought. The date is postponed another two or three months, and the patient begins to learn that he is one of those people who will not have the colostomy closed. This gradual adjustment works very well because there are colostomies that are temporary and are closed, and patients have heard of people who had temporary colostomies closed. Man is so adaptable that caring for a colostomy becomes just another routine for him; in time he will carry on his activities with little consciousness of an infirmity.

In terminal cancer when the patient is not told, the family is told of the hopelessness of the outlook: that the disease has gone so far that it cannot be aided by either surgery or radio-therapy, the two most important modalities we have in our fight against cancer at the present time. The family should then be told that experimental drugs are being used now and new surgical procedures being tried in attempts to control cancer; that to date these have not proven curative, but have in many instances prolonged life and reduced pain and suffering. It is necessary to stress these new attempts because the relatives, if told that nothing more can be done, are left alone. As they see it, the medical profession has washed its hands of this patient's disease. As a result, they begin hunting about for that will-o'-the-wisp, a cancer cure, which today we do not have, and pretty soon they will hear about doctors who do cure cancer. They will either find themselves rushing from pillar to post, giving the patient no rest at all, in looking for this magic, or will land in the hands of a charlatan who promises results while he impoverishes the family. On the other hand, if the relatives learn about the experimental methods being carried out in orthodox medical centers, and that the patient may be admitted for such care, if that is their wish, they feel that the medical profession is still interested. A family, so informed, will escape the pitfalls of the alluring promises of dishonest cancer "cures."

Treatment of a patient does not follow a constant set of rules. As the disease changes, as the patient's faculties change with it, as the family's attitude changes, truths, too, change, and the doctor demonstrates his ability by reacting to the ever new environment. No doctor will be right each time. He can take advice, he can read about the care of patients in such situations, but he must create in the crucible of his own mind an amalgam of all that information with the person he is. Then and only then what comes out of him will be authentic and meaningful to the patient; only then will he have acquired the wisdom needed for dealing with the sick.

There is no easy answer to the question, "Should the patient know the truth?" In most instances the physician's relation to the patient is an earnest, honest, and truthful one. In the few instances where truth and honesty would add hardships for the patient, the doctor must come to a decision by considering the patient rather than give room to his own philosophic notion about what is the moral way to live. The patient comes to a doctor a helpless person. He has no way of measuring the doctor's ability. He has only the faith, grown from previous experience, that physicians are, as a rule, to be trusted with the care of their patients. It is the physician's duty, therefore, to serve his patient best and salve his own conscience at some other time.

Mark Twain,[2] in his short story "Was it Heaven? Or

Hell?" tells of a pair of women who felt strongly about the evils of lying. When their doctor asks them whether they would tell a lie to shield a person from an undeserved injury or shame, their answer is "No."

"Not even a friend?"

"No."

"Not even your dearest friend?"

"No."

"Not even to save him from bitter pain and misery and grief?"

"No. Not even to save his life."

"Nor his soul?"

"Nor his soul."

"I ask you both—why?"

"Because to tell such a lie, or any lie, is a sin, and could cost us the loss of our own souls—*would,* indeed, if we died without time to repent."

The doctor's final response is: "Is such a soul as that *worth* saving? Reform! Drop this mean and sordid and selfish devotion to the saving of your shabby little souls, and hunt up something to do that's got some dignity to it! *Risk* your souls. risk them in good causes; then if you lose them, why should you care? Reform!"

REFERENCES

1. Frost, Robert: Bravado. Complete Poems of Robert Frost. New York, Henry Holt and Company, Inc., 1949.
2. Mark Twain: Was It Heaven? Or Hell? The Writings of Mark Twain, Vol. 24. New York, Harper & Brothers Publishers.

SHOULD THE PATIENT KNOW THE TRUTH?

The Magnificence of Understanding

By Ilse S. Wolff, R.N., M.A.

The question, "Should the patient know the truth?" obscures, in the categorical way it is put, the issue at hand. It is posed as if there were an either-or solution which would be binding and fitting for everyone. If in the realm of physical medicine we were asked, "What is better for the patient, medical treatment or surgery?" we would, at once, consider it a naive question.

We know from our study of human needs, human reactions, and human defenses that what might be beneficial for one person might be poison for another. In order to take a stand on such a question, we have to know what the patient is like, what it is that he wants. Our clues would have to come from the individual person.

Our second question would have to be who the person is who shall pass on the truth about a bleak or fatal diagnosis and prognosis. This person, in a very pertinent sense, is part of the situation. No ready-made answer or firm conviction will absolve him of the need of having his own position worked through. He must have come to terms with the drama of human existence and its finiteness, and with the facts of separation, loss, tragedy, and mortality.

It is generally agreed that the person to share diagnosis and prognosis with the patient is the doctor, and that it is within his discretion to decide how much the patient should be told. Yet nurses feel that this does not relieve them entirely of a responsibility. One has only to be present in study groups or professional discussions among nurses of the most varied fields to be convinced that this question is one which gives nurses a great deal of concern. The words may differ but the situation quoted is mostly one like this: "What do you do if the patient keeps asking you about his prognosis and the doctor evades the question or gives definite orders that his patient is not to be told about his condition and chances?"

A situation like this and similar ones present three problems. One is in the area of inter-disciplinary relationships and ethical precepts; the second has to do with the nurse's own conflicting feelings about a hopeless disease, a bleak prognosis, and death itself; the third is how to tell the truth to the patient, if that is indicated, in a way that is comforting and helps him to acceptance.

The first conflict does not seem too hard to resolve. The doctor-nurse relationship has lost a good deal of its old military rigidity and is acquiring more and more the character of a partnership. But even where that is not quite so, where a formal "upper-under relationship" prevails, the nurse is under a professional obligation to report observations which she, who is with the patient much longer and more continuously than the doctor, is able to make. Her observations about reactions to treatment, response to drug therapy, the functioning of body processes are appreciated as one of her most specific contributions to the patient's care and welfare. Her observing and reporting of emotional reactions might, in former times, have been deemed less appropriate and less objective in a scientific sense. With today's greater respect for emotions as reality factors, this differentiation should hardly exist.

The nurse who observes that her patient ponders and broods about his condition must share her observation with the physician who may see the patient too infrequently to be aware of this. In situations of this kind, a mature nurse may be of real help to the physician, be it that he feels not prepared for the answer the patient is seeking, or that he does not have the time and inner concentration for such a deep-reaching discussion, or not the close relationship to the patient that would make the discussion fruitful.

From all observations, it would seem that the problem of inter-disciplinary relationships is usually, if unconsciously, used as a smoke screen to hide and to suppress the real one. Let us forget, therefore, in our considerations who carries the ultimate responsibility in this area. What do we, as nurses, feel to be the patient's rights? What does he want if he asks us, in a direct or in a roundabout way, about his condition and his chances? How can we best contribute to the peace of declining months or weeks?

The temptation is great to answer these questions in a definite personal vein. Anything which has to do so intimately with the universal human condition cannot fail to touch off responses tinged heavily with one's own emotions and needs. We might be so threatened by the thought of death and so unable to face and admit its finality, that we may rationalize that the patient is unable to take it, that the shock would cause him to give up prematurely or to spend the time left to him in a constant depression. By reasoning and projecting in this way, we confuse identities. While reacting in self-protection by every means at our disposal, by diversion, evasion, denial, we may easily leave the patient in a virtual isolation, an aloneness in times of greatest need.

A young nurse told about her failure to break through the barrier of aloneness of a patient who was in the late stages of a bacterial endocarditis. Every day when she entered his room, she felt a strong upsurge of feelings of guilt. She was going to live while he, of her own age, was about to die. "I know he wanted to talk to me; but I always turned it into something light, a little joke, or into some evasive reassurance which had to fail. The patient knew and I knew. But, as he saw my desperate attempts to escape and felt my anxiety, he took pity on me and kept to himself what he wanted to share with another human being. And so he died and did not bother me."

Living through this experience, with its bitter aspects of guilt and failure, helped one young nurse to grow up professionally and to give to other patients what she had failed to give to this one. We know that there must be a better way of preparing nurses to face such harassing and difficult conflicts. Textbooks on the practice of nursing offer little assistance; they usually do not go beyond some general statements about what the nurse "ought" to feel or "ought" to be, in order to be of help. As the first intimate meeting with death usually leaves a deep mark on any nurse, it would seem appropriate that she be helped to absorb this experience by allowing her to express and explore her feelings with her teacher or counselor. The comprehending of such an event should not be left to a young inexperienced nurse alone or to the slow process of maturation.

Not every nurse matures under the impact of such an experience. The seemingly hardboiled and cynical way in which many a nurse talks about death is often the only defense she can put up against a feeling of helplessness and a vague generalized anxiety. In all these cases, the nurse's own conflicts and uncertainties make her unable to stay with the patient in his time of need. Her own needs block her sensitivity and her potential for helping. Because the patient will unfailingly pick up this atmosphere of fear and withdrawal and will respond to it with a withdrawal of his own, a great chance of giving comfort and a sense of human fellowship is lost. Here Robert Frost's [1] sad words become true:

> No, from the time when one is sick to death
> One is alone. . . . .

Nearly the same thing happens when the nurse is a partisan for telling, under all circumstances, the truth, the whole truth, and nothing but the truth. Again, the needs of the patient are bypassed, and the nurse's own needs take precedence. A differentiating line needs to be drawn between what I decide for myself and how I respond to the patient who definitely is "not I." I might say for myself that I would wish to know the truth, that everybody has a right to be confronted with the facts essential for his existence. Even if we could know our own selves well enough to be sure that we would still think and feel this way when facing a very bitter truth, this does not entitle us to deal with the patient as if he was "I" or the generalized personality of some doctrine. Preconceived theories, especially when they have strong emotional meaning for us, may actually blind us to what the patient's thoughts and feelings are and to what he asks us in words, gestures, glances, and silence.

If this is discussed, nurses nearly always justify their attitude with some painful, emotionally heavily charged experience of their own lives; they recall circumstances surrounding the death of a parent, a close friend, someone near and dear. Thus, the still unrelieved anxiety, the hurt and pain belonging to this event, confuses the nurse in her role and leads to a response in personal terms. This is humanly understandable. But for a nurse it means giving up her professional attitude and reacting in the way a lay person would; she also loses sight of her patient and becomes unable to tap the resources and appraise the limitations of his hidden strength.

We will be on safest ground, if we can take our clues from the patient himself. And we do receive clues, once we have been able to examine and accept our own attitudes about death, are reasonably free from anxiety and fears of our own, and ready for a sensitive perception of the patient's communications.

Some patients tell us unmistakably what they want and show us rather clearly the extent of their inner fortitude. An impressive example of current times was the matter-of-fact courage with which Senator Taft accepted the diagnosis of a quickly metastasizing malignancy and his fatal prognosis. From the reports given, we can deduct that he met his fate with objectivity, interested in hearing and appraising all the facts and prepared to be in charge of his own decisions to the last conscious minute. His story became known because he was in the limelight of public life. There are thousands of unknown people who in their own way hold the same attitude and can claim the same right.

Stephen Vincent Benet, in his short story "No Visitors"[2] tells how the hero, John Blagden, a writer, apparently after an exploratory operation, discovers during the span of a day the truth about his fatal condition; in this, he gets no help from either doctor or nurse. The nurse responds with the "don't you worry" technic, and the surgeon answers with evasions. This reassures momentarily, but after a short time Blagden begins to reverberate "the tone, the inflection of the voice," to analyze "the fine poised smile . . . the verdict written all over him." He comes to his conclusions at the end of the day: "Why, it is easy to do. . . . They make a great fuss about it, but it's easy to do. . . . All it takes is being mortal." Benet's patient has lived richly and positively and possesses the inner resources to face death as the rounding out of his life. But the people entrusted with his care do not credit him for the strength he has; in spite of his very direct questions, the patient has to struggle through it alone, unaided and even led far afield.

Not every patient will express himself so clearly, and many patients do not want to face their truth. It will require the nurse's full capacity for empathy, for feeling one's way into the patient, to receive the messages and to appraise their meaning. Some patients show through their behavior, through interest in their drugs and treatments, through their plans and preoccupations, that they don't want to be told, though the knowledge of their condition may be close to the surface of consciousness. That way, they may feel, they are best able to preserve equilibrium. To force any knowledge, not demanded or not clearly demanded, upon such a person will be an unkind, insensitive act. As Willard L. Sperry[8] says:

> Speaking the truth in love may mean at times keeping silence.

This is especially true with the patient who has cancer. The very word seems to spell terror and doom for many people and is avoided. Words like tumor, swelling, lump, or growth, and sometimes even sarcoma, the deeper but, to the laity, less known form of cancer, are used as substitutes. This in itself is telling. Take, for instance, the following recent case. An old experienced laboratory technician, seen for her angina pectoris, trusted the public health nurse only after several weeks so far as to uncover her breast; showing an egg-sized cancerous tumor, ready to break down, the patient insisted, "Don't say it; I know it." In later contacts, it was found out that she was extremely sensitive to "talks behind her back" about her having cancer. Cancer was synonymous with living death, with losing one's physical integrity, with being repulsive to oneself and others. And, living with it, as this woman did in a furnished, fourth-floor room, absolutely and helplessly alone, might have well been a "poisoning secret," as C. G. Jung puts it, a reality too much dreaded to be dealt with alone. In this case the patient after a while unburdened herself. She could do so because the public health nurse showed that she cared yet was not afraid and was willing to let the patient take the lead.

Many patients have to get ready for their truth. To recognize that, to stay with the patient and to respond to his requests in a sensitive manner, is a far cry from a categorical conviction about what the patient ought or ought not to be told. Such an attitude stems from a respect for the individual who loses none of his prerogatives and his dignity by being a patient and having a possibly fatal disease. He remains "the captain of his soul" and can choose what he wants to discuss and what not.

It would be a mistake to oversimplify this. Nothing is clearcut in decisions of this kind. Our strongest feelings are usually ambivalent. Things tend to look quite different under the sober light of the midmorning from what they look in the lonely hours of the night. Pain and fatigue are great conditioners and influencers, and the nurse may find her patient feel and react differently from one day to the next. If she is willing to follow rather than lead, to participate rather than decide, to respond rather than interpret, she will find it easier to steer through those uncharted regions; they will be uncharted in every single case, because no two cases will ever be alike.

How can the nurse attain such an attitude of sensitive response, of entering into the feelings of her patient rather than avoiding or directing them? Her helpfulness rests upon two foundations. The one is whatever fortitude and conviction her own philosophy of life can give her, and the other is an honest and courageous stock-taking of her reactions to whatever truth her patients (and ultimately she herself) are faced with. If she tries sincerely to become familiar with her own reactions, her own threshold of endurance and strength, and her own anxieties, she is in much less danger of considering her way of feeling as the universal one and of projecting its implications upon others. In recognizing her own fears, she stands a better chance of controlling them and of protecting her patient from their manifestations. This does not mean that the "fear and trembling" of which the Bible speaks will not often be her part, the price she has to pay for her privilege of accompanying a patient through the dark valleys of the shadow; but it means that the irrational anxiety which clouds perception and paralyzes strength can be overcome.

Her own specific and personal convictions, the basis for her own relationship with mortality, are the source of her strength. Again, it is essential that there is no confusion of identities, and that the nurse is aware that her philosophic and religious outlook belongs to herself and cannot be offered to the patient. The temptation is great to offer to others the consolation of convictions grown in the garden of one's own life, nurtured from the experiences and revelations of a lifetime. Yet the meaning of life and death is expressed differently and in different symbols. Frequently the nurse will be able to leave this function to the clergyman, but there are patients without formal religious affiliation and moments when the situation calls for a spontaneous, immediate reaction on her part.

One hesitates to give examples of how the nurse can express herself in such cases constructively, as this expression must be her own or it would not be true, not helpful. Any nurse with this responsibility will have to struggle for the right word or gesture in each individual case, but when the foundations are solidly laid, she will find the words to express them. Often we find there is not much need for words; feeling will communicate itself, and emotion will respond to emotion.

In this light, the question, "Should the patient know the truth?" changes to the challenge, "Am I ready and willing to be with the patient on his last road, willing to accept his feelings, different as they might be from mine, willing to respect equally his wish to be told or to be spared?" Only when we are free for both, is it true what Walt Whitman[4] says:

> The faithful hand of the living
> does not desert the hand of the dying.

REFERENCES

1. FROST, ROBERT: Home Burial. Complete Poems of Robert Frost. New York, Henry Holt and Company, Inc., 1949.
2. BENET, STEPHEN VINCENT: No Visitors. Selected Works of Stephen Vincent Benet. New York, Copyright, 1940, by Stephen Vincent Benet.
3. SPERRY, W. L.: The Ethical Basis of Medical Practice. New York, Paul B. Hoeber, Inc., 1950.
4. WHITMAN, WALT: To Think of Time. An Anthology of Famous English and American Poetry. New York, The Modern Library, 1944.

The Patient Speaks

By Martin G. Goldner, M.D.

The patient should not be left out in a discussion which concerns no one more than him. Indeed, "the truth of the matter" will determine his life, his future welfare or happiness; the problem is how much is he to know of what the days to come might bring to him. He is not only the object but the true partner of this discussion; he is the one who raises the question silently or openly; he is the one whose life or death will seal the truth, whether he was told so or not.

The physician, mindful of the Hippocratic oath to serve his patient to the best of his knowledge and ability and to protect him against harm, finds himself in a dilemma if *telling* the truth of his diagnosis and prognosis may increase the patient's fear and anguish. He turns for advice to the clergy, the lawyer, and the philosopher. He might do well to turn also to the patient and learn from him whether *withholding* the truth may not sometimes increase fear and anguish, jeopardize contentment and thus be harmful. Many records are left to us in the literature by patients who have lived through the dilemma of this question. Only two shall be presented here. They come from unusual men, but should not be considered as exceptions. It seems rather that the special gifts of these men enabled them to express not only their own feelings and reactions but also those of thousands of other patients who silently went through the same experience.

Franz Rosenzweig, philosopher and religious thinker (1886-1929), was not quite 35 years old when he noticed the first symptoms of his disease. He suddenly and without noticeable cause lost control of his legs, fell down a staircase, and experienced difficulties in swallowing; his speech became slurred. All this occurred in repeated episodes. His physicians soon recognized the true nature of his affliction, amyotrophic lateral sclerosis, incurable and fatal then as it is now. Within a few months the disease progressed rapidly. Short remissions were followed by more severe exacerbations. After not more than one year, the patient was left as a spastic quadruplegic, unable to talk and capable of swallowing only with the greatest difficulty. During this period his physicians tried to give him hope and attempted, against their better knowledge, to convince him that recovery and cure could be expected. Since all clinical experience indicated that the end was near, they believed that they could spare their patient the truth. Contrary to all expectation, the patient survived for nine years. This is what he had to say about the initial period of his illness:[1]

> At first all that I knew about my disease I knew instinctively. I knew it even before my physician had made the diagnosis. Then I tried to have my notions confirmed. Intentionally I made my inquiries only in general terms, so that I would not get false information. My physician made full use of the opportunities to deceive me that I gave him by simply not putting any questions to him. In this respect he has not overlooked anything. Some time later when he was on vacation he wrote me a long letter imploring me not to give up hope. He described in detail the gradual improvement in my condition which should

> be expected. It was only then that I became frightened not for myself, but on account of the consequences which such sympathetic professional lies could have in other cases where the patient might believe in them. Place yourself in my situation and try to imagine how much more I would have suffered had I believed him. Each small progression and aggravation of the process, as it occurred then week by week, would have increased my desperation. Only my better insight and resignation permitted me to bear the disease then as now.

And some time later the patient had this to say about the nature of his illness:[2]

> The words pain and suffering which you use seem quite odd to me. A condition into which one has slithered gradually, and consequently got used to, is not suffering but simply a condition—a condition that leaves room for joy and suffering like any other . . . What must appear suffering when seen from the outside is actually only a sum of great difficulties that have to be overcome.

How many patients like him ask anxiously not only for help but also for truthfulness? How many could tell the truth to their physician, and how many would be able to adjust to their condition better, even if it is a "state of gradually declining life," if they only were told that no other way is open.

Franz Rosenzweig continued to cope with the ever increasing sum of difficulties which his illness put in his way. He remained active and productive in the face of approaching death for nine long years. He died of a short and fulminant supervening pneumonia.

Hans Zinsser, physician and great scientist, noticed suddenly, when he was in his sixties, a suspicious and unexplainable paleness and a slight yellowish tinge in his skin. A well-trained sportsman, he began to feel weak and to lose his stamina. He made his own tentative diagnosis: leukemia. Then he went to see his physician and had the diagnosis confirmed. This is what he wrote in his autobiographical novel, "As I Remember Him,"[8] in which he speaks of himself in the third person as R.S.

> This friend to whom R.S. had gone was one of those precious individuals whom nature had meant to be physicians. He was fond of R.S. and showed it most helpfully by his affectionate abstinence from any expression of sympathy. Together with his good friend he stood for a long time at the office window . . . but in those minutes, R.S. told me, something took place in his mind that he regarded as a sort of compensatory adjustment to the thought that he would soon be dead. In the prospect of death, life seemed to be given a new meaning and fresh poignancy. It seemed, he said, from that moment as though all that his heart felt and his senses perceived were taking on a "deep autumnal tone" and increased vividness. From then on, instead of being saddened, he found, to his own delighted astonishment, that his sensitiveness to the simplest experiences even for things that in other years he might hardly have noticed was infinitely enhanced.
>
> As his disease caught up with him, R.S. felt increasingly grateful for the fact that death was coming to him with due warning and gradually. Always he had thought that rapid and unexpected extinction would be most merciful. But now he was thankful that he had time to compose his spirit and to spend a last year in affectionate and actually merry association with those dear to him.

No doubt these two men faced the truth of a fatal disease as not every patient can do it. No doubt most physicians will seek a course lying between the two extremes chosen by the physicians of Franz Rosenzweig and of Hans Zinsser. And undoubtedly telling the truth is not always the pronouncement of a death sentence as in these two instances. This alone goes to show that the answer to the question "Should the patient know the truth?" cannot be a simple yes or no, that our question is not merely an abstract, legal, ethical, or philosophical one, nor a question of fact, but foremost a question of human relations, of living men. It arises between people who meet not as seekers of the truth but under quite specific circumstances: as patient and physician, as the one who seeks help and the one who promises to give help to the best of his knowledge and ability. Help and truth are not the same. Perhaps the truth of the physician's knowledge and ability may be all the help which is needed. He may truthfully be able to promise relief and recovery. Then the question poses no problems. But when the truth appears to be that the physician's knowledge and ability cannot bring the help expected of him, that cure is not in his power, is he to keep this truth away from his patient? Cannot such truth bring help too, though not physical help? Is the patient indeed better off if he lives blindly and with false hopes? It is possible and seems likely that what R.S. experienced in his last year of life is not really unique but paralleled by the experiences of many others. Often it may be better for the patient to face openly even a grave fate rather than remain uncertain and plagued by the ever-growing suspicion of being left out alone from a knowledge that is shared by many others whom it concerns less than himself. Are we correct to assume, as we do so often, that our patients will feel more secure if denied the knowledge of the seriousness of their condition? R.S. praises his physician as helpful because he refrains from expressing sympathy. Franz Rosenzweig has a similar thought in one of his letters:[2]

> Parsons and doctors should not take a sentimental view of death; they are companions of the dying man, not mere bystanders. Sentimentality is proper for the bystanders. The dying themselves are not sentimental. And the bystanders are the less so, the less they are mere bystanders.

Both men expect the physician to be understanding and responsive to the needs of the patient. They expect trust and confidence that must be mutual. In the case of chronic diseases, may they be fatal or not, such truthfulness seems to be essential. The chronically ill patient, like Franz Rosenzweig, catches up soon with false consolations and empty promises. If told of the probable seriousness of his future, he will be more appreciative of the little help which the physician still can offer, and more cooperative in following all suggestions to prepare himself for the ever growing "sum of difficulties" into which chronic disease transmutes. This applies to the patient crippled by arthritis or paralyzed by a stroke, to the patient likely to lose his eyesight or the power of his voice. This also applies to the patient "doomed" by a spreading malignant disease. Some will respond as Hans Zinsser did, others remain confident in the knowledge that the physician is at their side in the battle against death—and still others will become active co-workers in the struggle which will change the sad truth of today into a good one of tomorrow.

What, after all, is this truth which we can hide or give? It is conditioned by the limits of our knowledge and ability; it may change not only with the changing and increasing proficiency of medical science but also with unexpected and unforeseeable turns in the natural course of diseases. If the physician realizes that all his truthfulness does not empower him to pronounce ultimate and inescapable sentences, and if the patient recognizes that the physician's answer is not a final judgment, then the confidence between physician and patient will not be overtaxed when the truth is told.

REFERENCES

1. Rosenzweig, F.: Briefe, edited by Edith Rosenzweig. Berlin, Schocken Verlag, 1935.
2. Glatzer, N. N.: Franz Rosenzweig, His Life and Thought. New York, Schocken Books, Inc., Copyright 1953.
3. Zinsser, H.: As I Remember Him. Boston, Little, Brown and Company, 1939.

What Patient, What Truth?*

By Bernard C. Meyer, M.D.

And oftentimes to win us to our harm
The instruments of darkness tell us truths,
Win us with honest trifles to betray us
In deepest consequence.
Shakespeare: MACBETH

Should the patient know the truth? What patient, let us hasten to ask, and what truth? For it is certain that there exists no general dictum or prescription for this troubled aspect of the communications between a physician and his patient. What is good medicine for the one may prove catastrophic for another. Indeed, the only rule whereby the doctor may be wisely guided is for him to know the facts, know his patient, and know himself.

The doctor is more than a diagnostician and a healer. He is a bearer of tidings of salvation and doom, upon whose word hang the hope and the despair, the joy and the woe of sick and frightened patients and their kin. Grown men behold the doctor as some composite parent, hero, and demi-god—a conception of which the doctor himself may prove at times to be an eager exponent. Thus endowed with attributes of omnipotence and omniscience it behooves him to use that power with wisdom and re-

* Reprinted, with permission, from Journal of the Mount Sinai Hospital *20*: 344,1954.

straint, for should he be one of the lonely tormented souls who have entered into the domain of healing to satisfy some secret yearning to direct and control those fellow beings of whom he is covertly afraid, his words may prove to be both intemperate and noxious. Such a doctor is given to pronouncements of the "truth" with an underlying essence of brutality, which he dubs "frankness." He dispenses counsel where angels might fear to tread. He advises the inhibited to engage in fleshly pleasures, prescribes matrimony for the perplexed, motherhood for the depersonalized, and Miami for the depressed. Indeed he is most dogmatic when he is most confused, for when he cannot be positive he most keenly feels his inner emptiness. He cannot permit his patient to leave without a diagnosis, without a prescription, nor without an injunction. For him the blurting of a reckless truth is an act of self-rescue. Possessed of minimal self-knowledge and hence a scant awareness of psychogenesis, he becomes irascible in the face of illnesses that stem from the spirit. Petulantly he accuses his patient of "just talking it into yourself," while angrily ordering him to "pull yourself together."

Truth, sir, is a cow which will yield skeptics
No more milk; so they have gone to milk the bull.
Samuel Johnson

The obsessional physician, on the other hand, meticulously addicted to a policy of dedicated honesty, finds it incumbent upon him to convey every fact and every finding. Perhaps this represents in some measure a legacy from his internship days when he feared the humiliation of having overlooked some physical sign detected by the hawk-eyed resident or chief of service. Perhaps he will be "shown up" again for overlooking some abnormality which a new consultant may mention to the patient. Whatever the basis for this insistent sharing of clinical detail, the presence of an untold number of functional murmurs of the heart has been communicated to an untold number of mothers, and not invariably in the absence of their children. Other pointless "truths" so confided embrace roentgenographic curiosities, mild deviations in the basal metabolic rate, questionable enlargements of ovaries, and debatably significant malpositions of the uterus.

Her taste exact for faultless fact amounts to a disease.
W. S. Gilbert: MIKADO

This commerce in "truth" finds its most widespread application in that baleful instrument, the sphygmomanometer under the aegis of which a sizable fraction of the civilized population is conspiring with some elements in the medical profession in running a "clinical" numbers racket. Figures of 140, 165, and 180 (the diastolic pressure is never cited) are bandied about by individuals who are scientifically unequipped to comprehend or assimilate the significance of the numbers yet utilize them as the framework of a hypochondriac picture. The matter is all the more lamentable since the definition of normal range of blood pressure is in itself open to question and subject to periodic revision. Save for exceptional instances, there would seem to be no more cogent excuse for revealing a blood pressure reading to a patient than his serum phosphatase.

There are other instances wherein the invention of diagnostic instruments and the discovery of scientific facts have contributed to the dissemination of medical myths under the guise of Hippocratic truth. Thus the discovery of the syndrome of acute appendicitis has given birth to that shadowy entity, the chronically diseased appendix which is treated periodically by a mysterious process called "freezing." The invention of the x-ray apparatus played a definite role in promoting the one-time cult of visceroptosis, inducing zealous purveyors of roentgenographic gospel to subject their patients to acrobatics and abdominal appliances, in an heroic endeavor to combat the malign effect of gravity upon stomach or colon.

In France, one gains the impression that the entire nation is afflicted with disease of the liver which on closer inspection proves to be but a transatlantic manifestation of a national malady of our own, attributed lately to vitamin deprivation, in the recent past to "acid in the blood," and in some quarters apparently to chronic barbiturate deficiency.

Truth does not so much good in the world as the semblance of it does evil.
La Rochefoucauld: Maxims, 1665

Another type is the physician who dispenses truth out of a process of psychologic projection. Wrestling with indifferent success against his own weaknesses, he may display great vigor in combatting the temptations of his patients. Struggling against his own voracity, he may, for the sake of companionship, impose stern dietary restrictions upon his marginally corpulent clientele. Such a basis for prescription may prove especially unfortunate when the doctor summons his patients to enlist in his own ascetic crusade. One shudders to remember the thousands of thirsty victims of angina pectoris of twenty and more years ago from whom whiskey was withheld because it had not yet been learned that alcohol by mouth is an excellent dilator of the coronary arteries.

A more merciful attitude was displayed by that physician, who, having just forbidden his cardiac patient indulgence in tobacco, alcohol and amorous intimacies, was asked by the victim, "Tell me, doctor, if I give these things up will I live longer?" To which his physician replied with charm and candor, "No, but it'll seem longer."

It does seem perplexing that so many people are still alive today, who, fifty years ago, were given but six months to live by doctors long since passed away. One cannot doubt that some of these dire pronouncements were indeed uttered by truth-tellers with a penchant for prophecy, but the suspicion is warranted that many of these recollections are narcissistic chortlings by hypochondriacs; these elderly ladies and gentlemen have ever delighted in proving everyone wrong, even though it involves misquoting a physician who, no longer on hand to dispute the accuracy, has ascribed to him a pronouncement he never made, or at least never in so vulnerable a fashion.

On the other hand, there are "truths" known to patients which merit attention and respect, even when they appear absurd in the face of esteemed scientific data. An eminent surgeon, in the early days of his practice, was told by a subject for hemorrhoidectomy that he would die, if operated upon. The doctor, despite confidence in his appraisal of the patient's health and his own skill, postponed the operation and reinvestigated thoroughly the man's physical status. Being fully pursuaded that there was no medically discernible contraindication to this minor procedure, the surgeon performed the operation, whereupon the patient died forthwith. The autopsy failed to disclose any cause for death.

Psychiatrists are fully cognizant of the inexorable and

unswerving pursuit of self-destruction consciously sought for and successfully attained by those unfortunate souls imprisoned in a hell of dark despair. The most vigilant effort proves often vain in thwarting the resourcefulness of a person determined on suicide. Nor is there reason to suppose that a less conscious will to die is any less powerful; our scientifically attained truths to the contrary, it is wise to heed the voice of him who prophesies his own demise. Not long ago, I urged a panic-stricken young man, suffering from a chronic pulmonary affliction, to relax a nightly vigil maintained by him in the shape of an orthopneic fright. His physician had advised me that the respiratory distress was out of proportion to the existing disease, and I assumed that his nocturnal anxiety was a defense against a fear of dying. I assured him he would not die, promising him that his yielding to a much-needed sleep was devoid of danger. He must have been persuaded of this glib truth, for he was dead within thirty-six hours.

The truth you speak doth lack some gentleness
And time to speak it in; you rub the sore,
When you should bring the plaster.

Shakespeare: THE TEMPEST

A happier case was that of a young man with a pulmonary abscess who had served under fire in the Polish, French, and American armies during World War II and been repeatedly subjected to real threats of annihilation. He asserted with conviction that he would perish were he operated upon. Persuasion and reassurance were of no avail. Upon my recommendation, the surgeons, ever loath to operate upon an individual so minded, waited. This was his story: While in the American army he had fallen in love with a Dutch girl whom he made pregnant and then married. Now he was faced with two choices: to emigrate at once to the United States to be joined later by his wife after the birth of her child, or to remain with her until that event that they might all travel together to begin life anew on these shores. He favored the latter, but his wife urged him to go alone, which advice he reluctantly followed. Some months later he learned that a son was born, and not long thereafter that following a respiratory ailment the child had died. He grieved greatly over this, all the more because he felt that, had he been on hand, his contacts with American army doctors might have saved his son's life. The mere recital of this tale appeared to dispel his gloomy thoughts. No effort was made to emphasize that he like his son had a respiratory ailment and that he too must therefore die. A day or two later he confided that he had given up the "foolish ideas." Whereupon he was operated upon and did not die. I am not suggesting that death would have proved inevitable, had he been operated upon at the outset. I do know, however, that experienced surgeons shy away from such undertakings if this is at all possible.

Some of us shrink from imparting an unqualified truth because we are reluctant to become a bearer of ill tidings. In ancient times, it is said, messengers bringing news of defeat from the field of battle were put to death. So today, a physician may avoid conveying unpleasant news lest he evoke a storm of woe and hatred in others, and one of guilt within himself. There are facts, however, that must be told. If a leg or a breast must be sacrificed, the patient must be told, though never tactlessly. The untoward effect of concealing or gilding such truths was clearly understood and described by Victor Rosen [1] who was obliged to play the role of messenger in behalf of surgeons who could not bring themselves to tell a lady of 55, afflicted with a saddle embolus of the aorta, that she would have to lose her left leg below the mid thigh. Faced with well-intentioned evasion the patient entered into a state of dangerous manic excitement which ended abruptly as soon as she heard the true, albeit tragic, facts. Not long thereafter, gangrenous changes appeared in the other leg, and again the surgeons, knowing that amputation of that leg too would prove necessary, hesitated to tell her so. Again, symptoms of excitement appeared in the patient who suspected that all was not well. When informed finally that the second leg would have to be removed, she quieted down and, after a day or so of depression and agitation, recovered her usual equanimity. "I knew it all the time," she said, "it didn't look good to me. Why don't they (the surgeons) tell me?" When it was explained that the surgeons were naturally reluctant to bear such unhappy tidings, she exclaimed, "What have they to be unhappy about—it's my leg!"

My tongue hath but a heavier tale to say
I play the torturer, by small and small,
To lengthen out the worst that must be spoken.

Shakespeare: RICHARD II

The likelihood of the eventual unfolding of the truth from one source or another, makes it often advisable to acquaint a patient with the facts as directly and simply as possible. This is true as a rule for such long illnesses of uncertain prognosis as multiple sclerosis. Here again, concealing of the truth may not only nourish anxiety with growing doubt but may also interfere with the capacity of the patient to make an adjustment to a new reality.

Most vexing is the matter of truth and cancer. In general, two attitudes prevail, to tell all and to tell nothing. Statistics furnished to prove the soundness of the "tell all" position,[2] appear to be of limited value. There is a story about a well known urologic surgeon who was hospitalized for a hypernephroma, which diagnosis had been withheld from him. One day, he confided in the interne, explaining that there was no reason why he, a mature man and an experienced surgeon, should not be told the truth. The interne, caught off guard, confessed the ominous diagnosis, whereupon the surgeon-patient, taking advantage of a momentary absence of a nurse, leapt to his death. The aim of a fixed policy must be directed not at some patients, nor at most patients, but at all patients, and an occasional failure condemns the entire policy. On the other hand, those who practice not telling often deal in anxiety-provoking evasion and subterfuge. They hint to a patient that he has "a bad tumor," and become naively irascible if the word *cancer* is mentioned. Moreover, an established reputation for not telling may backfire, leading even non-cancer patients to doubt a diagnosis of benign adenoma. Some surgeons have found it useful to inform their patients that the excised lesion was precancerous—that had it remained in situ it would have turned into cancer—a practice which appears satisfactory in many instances.

It is evident that there can be no policy at all, for policy implies uniformity, and uniformity is a distillate of indolence and insensitivity that has no place in the practice of medicine. The doctor must know his patient; there is no other way. If a doctor believes that he himself cannot get this knowledge, he should seek help. As a rule this is neither desirable nor practical; a humane physician, devoting as much time to the patient as to the lesion, can mostly discern a proper course of action. Patients often provide broad hints that they do not want to know. A 63 year old lady, suffering from a rectal cancer, delayed consulting a physician for six months after the onset of rectal bleeding. By explaining that she thought it was her menstrual flow, although this had ceased some seven years before, she made it abundantly clear that she was unwilling to face reality, and that when confronted by unpleasant and fearsome occurrences she was quite capable of dealing successfully with them through a process of denial. On the other hand, following a radical mastectomy for cancer, a surgeon following his usual practice of not telling, disregarded a husband's advice to inform his wife of the diagnosis. The husband pleaded in vain with the surgeon who dismissed him with a "we know better." He was wrong. The patient, a sensitive and perceptive person, feeling herself surrounded by duplicity and evasion, and assailed by uncertainty and doubt, became depressed and agitated; only when she ultimately learned the truth, did her spirits regain their former buoyancy. Now she knew with what she had to cope and could fight for her life against an identified foe.

Even more painful decisions confront the physician whose patient is on the threshold of death. Here again no unswerving custom will avail, for there are those who, when told of the certitude of imminent death, receive this word with a sudden tranquility and calm which mercifully replaces the anguished terror of a hopeless hope. Writing on this issue of truth, L. K. Henderson [3] observed:

> The idea that the truth, the whole truth, and nothing but the truth can be conveyed to the patient is an example of false abstraction, of that fallacy called by

Whitehead "The fallacy of misplaced concreteness." It results from neglecting factors that cannot be excluded from the concrete situation and that have an effect that cannot be neglected. Another fallacy also is involved, the belief that it is not too difficult to know the truth; but of this I will not speak further.

I beg that you will not suppose that I am recommending, for this reason, that you should always lie to your patients. Such a conclusion from what I have said would correspond roughly to a class of fallacies that I have already referred to above. Since telling the truth is impossible, there can be no sharp distinction between what is true and what is false. But surely that does not relieve the physician of his moral responsibility. On the contrary the difficulties that arise from the immense complexity of the phenomena do not diminish but rather increase the moral responsibility of the physician, and one of my objects has been to describe the facts through which the nature of that moral responsibility is determined.

Far older than the precept, "the truth, the whole truth, and nothing but the truth," is another that originates within our profession, that has always been the guide of the best physicians, and, if I may venture a prophecy, will always remain so: "So far as possible, do no harm." You can do harm by the process that is quaintly called telling the truth. You can do harm by lying. In your relations with patients you will inevitably do much harm, and this will be by no means confined to your strictly medical blunders. It will also arise from what you say and what you fail to say. But try to do as little harm as possible, not only in treatment with drugs, or with the knife, but also in treatment with words, with the expression of your sentiments and emotions. Try at all times to act upon the patient so as to modify his sentiments to his own advantage, and remember that, to this end, nothing is more effective than arousing in him the belief that you are concerned wholeheartedly and exclusively for his welfare.

REFERENCES

1. Rosen, V.: The role of denial in acute post-operative affective reactions following removal of body parts. Psychosom. Med. *12*:356, 1950.
2. Kelly, W. D., and Friesen, S. R.: Do cancer patients want to be told? Surgery *27*:822, 1950.
3. Henderson, H. J.: Physician and patient as a social system. New Eng. J. Med. *112*:819, 1935.

The Part of Disease That is Fear

By Samuel Z. Orgel, M.D.

Illness is the great leveler of men. It exposes their fears, insecurities, and dependencies. This chapter is concerned with the emotional disturbance that affects patients with serious disease. Such a disturbance may be the result of the patient's fear of death, incapacity, or pain and suffering. It is a misfortune when these disturbances arise needlessly from incorrect ideas about the future course of the disease. A grave prognosis may have been given in error by the doctor or misinterpreted by the patient; or perhaps the patient has a pessimistic conception of the outlook quite unknown to the doctor who therefore cannot correct it.

The most important aspect of our subject lies in the patient-doctor relationship; this expresses itself in two psychologic reactions which both depend upon the transference relationship that grows up between patient and doctor. In both the doctor comes to represent a good omnipotent parent, and both are positive in nature, but one is helpful and the other harmful to the progress of therapy. In one, the patient is compliant, trusts the doctor, and is therefore cooperative in the therapy. The other reaction, though positive, is nevertheless detrimental to progress because the patient regresses and becomes a helpless child completely dependent upon the doctor. He visits or phones him frequently, is constantly worried, asks many questions, doubts if he is carrying out correctly the doctor's orders, feels helpless and must be waited on constantly. By doing this he tends to prolong and aggravate his illness.

All illness has an intense psychologic effect. In transient illnesses it is considered of little importance. When, however, the disease seems to threaten one's life, or one's social or economic position, or one's hopes and ambitions, it becomes a matter of profound psychologic importance. The effects of great anxiety may vary with different people and different situations, but invariably anxiety about one's body tends to disturb the regulation of the autonomic nervous system and to aggravate the symptoms of the disease. When one's health seems to be seriously threatened, the most important and disabling symptom is a feeling of weakness and utter exhaustion bordering on collapse, quite out of proportion to the constitutional effects of the actual illness.

The patient's conception of the disease and its course, whether erroneous or not, determines in a large measure his psychologic reactions and thus modifies the symptoms which will result. The doctor can be greatly helped in assessing these symptoms by learning the patient's ideas about his trouble, especially what pain, suffering, and disability he anticipates. The patient's outlook, his faith in the doctor, and his fears have a remarkable effect on the course of all illness; these fears must and can be modified by the doctor's interest and explanations.

Doctors are aware of the great difficulties involved in conveying to an anxious patient an understanding of the significance of his illness. While the patient desires consciously to hear a favorable report, unconsciously he tends to take the pessimistic view. Patients though outwardly calm are inwardly afraid and disturbed and often fail to understand what the doctor may express simply and clearly. At times their anxiety and agitation may be so great that they have no idea at all of what was said. Later they will project their own instinctive fears in the doctor's mouth and attribute to him their own idea of the seriousness of the disease. This happens even with highly intelligent patients who then need to be told again and again about their symptoms and their illness. A physician noted for his ability to explain a patient's illness once told a successful, intelligent and apparently calm patient that he had but one slight chance in twenty of having serious trouble within the next year, yet on the following day the patient and his wife insisted that they had been informed that he had nineteen chances in twenty of dying within the year.

It is impossible to determine what one's own reaction will be to the belief that he has a fatal disease. It is difficult if not impossible for us to imagine living without an optimistic outlook and knowing that our life's course will inevitably be downward. Complete hopelessness has a highly morbific effect. Very few bear it with resignation. Most people refuse to accept it, question the diagnosis, and persist in seeking further advice and newer or different treatments. The most fortunate people, and there are some, bear it with fortitude and retain their interests in their activities and in other people. Some sick people become disagreeable, ugly and unpleasant, jealous of the health enjoyed by others, and angry that they themselves should be hopelessly ill; these unhappy people are difficult to help. Almost without exception, the sick patient loses energy and feels a lassitude, a weakness and fatigue bordering on exhaustion, symptoms that are due to his associated emotional disturbance and quite apart from the symptoms that may be caused directly by the disease.

On the other hand, there are people who bear fairly well the knowledge that a potentially serious disease is present as long as it causes few or no symptoms. These people will carry on in the optimistic belief that their trouble will be indefinitely delayed. Many accept the possibility of a fatal termination at an unknown time and work on calmly; others are worn down with agitation, depression, and exhaustion long before they begin to suffer materially from the disease itself.

The fear of incapacity is the greatest and most potent source of anxiety. Any symptom or minor lesion may be wrongly regarded by the patient as a possible early manifestation of a crippling disease, and therefore becomes a potential cause of an emotional upset. Patients are usually disappointed when the doctor seems to show little or no interest. To the surprise or annoyance of the physician, the patient sometimes becomes panicky and makes unreasonable demands for further investigation, consultation, and treatment. Many patients cannot bear to sit idly by while nothing is being done, believing that their disease will progress to disability. Occasionally, a patient may evidence anxiety and turmoil in an early stage of a serious disease, and later accept bravely the condition and real incapacity. Some other patients give up too readily and accept fatalistically a state of disability when active convalescent training would benefit them. Unfortunately, the little psychologic setbacks that occur during convalescence from prolonged disease are often interpreted by the patient as serious relapses and frequently cause unnecessary anxiety and prolonged morbidity.

Since we are aware of how the fear of discomfort and pain often aggravates the illness and causes needless symptoms, we can help patients with serious and even fatal diseases by supporting them and by promising relief from pain and suffering. A patient not knowing the usual course of his disease may magnify, in anticipation, the discomfort to be borne and have a natural but unfounded dread that it cannot be controlled. It is a helpful measure to correct at all times any false ideas about the suffering to be expected from diseases of all kinds, whatever the prognosis may be.

The physician must be certain of his diagnosis before telling a patient that he has a fatal disease. Seldom is anything lost by waiting, unless a patient's social and economic responsibilities demand that he have the knowledge at the earliest possible time. Even under such circumstances, the patient's activities in arranging his affairs can give him an interest that takes his attention away from himself and buffers the blow. When a hopeless diagnosis is certain, it should be told gradually, or it may be delayed until the patient senses the situation and indicates himself whether or not he wishes to be told. In telling the patient one should, if possible, use words that do not have a dreadful emotional significance for lay people.

It is interesting to note that some patients who were "neurotic" all their lives face serious illness with firmness and bravery. The occurrence of serious trouble removes their psychologic difficulties.

I cannot emphasize too strongly the importance of giving the patient with a serious disease a clear and concise understanding of his problems. This must be considered a vital part of the patient's treatment. Thus grave anxiety can often be prevented; when undue fear with its attendant symptoms is already present, the patient's understanding usually leads to prompt relief. Seldom does the patient attach the same meaning to words and terms as the doctor. It is of the utmost importance to speak in positive terms, to stress favorable things rather than to deny the likelihood of serious effects. The explanation must be based upon the doctor's firm conviction. If adequate explanations do not relieve the patient, we should look for emotional difficulties that are more deep-seated and not related to the structural disease.

It is necessary, then, for any physician to treat the patient psychologically and to assess his symptoms correctly. It is helpful to recognize and take into consideration his nature, his constitutional characteristics, and his reaction patterns. These factors may greatly modify his nervous response to disease just as they modify his physical reaction. Some people are constitutionally unable to endure suffering well; some feel the indignity of disease, loathe its ugliness, and cannot bear to be no longer attractive; some cannot stand to be out of things, to lose the prestige of activity, direction, and responsibility; some accept disease with resignation, some with fear; but many bear it bravely. The challenge of illness brings out the best and the worst traits of human character. But almost all patients can be helped by the physician who understands them, feels for them, attends to them, and tries to help them.

Special Problems in Psychiatric Nursing

By M. Olga Weiss, R.N., M.Litt.

For the psychiatric nurse the patient's knowing the truth has special meaning. She has the problem of taking care of persons who are in the hospital because the truth is not to their liking, is too painful for them to accept, or has even been twisted a bit to get them there. And further, nearly all persons are suspicious about entering a psychiatric hospital and about the procedures regulating life there.

I believe every patient should know the truth, within reason. It may knock him out at first, but having received the worst news, which probably he has sensed for a long time, he can recoup his forces; and while he must fight for recovery, he has a good firm starting place.

Telling the truth or being sure that the patient knows the truth does not mean going out of one's way to point out unpleasant facts about an illness; it does not mean being brutal. There is nothing to be gained by telling the senile patient that he is in the hospital because his brain isn't functioning normally, or telling an acutely disturbed schizophrenic patient that he is behaving badly. The immediate problem in a mental institution is to be reassuring and calm to a frightened and bewildered person. On the other hand, even though the patient may be quite disturbed, and may have been brought in forcefully, he should be told about the hospital; that he will be in a locked building, that there are certain unpleasing features, but that it need not be a permanent incarceration. All too often the loss of personal liberty in the locked building and even the loss of personal dignity is held over a patient as a threat or a taunt. These truths should not be kept from him, but they can be told quietly in a matter-of-fact tone and with courtesy.

Depending upon the patient's ability to understand what is taking place—and it is the nurse's responsibility to make every effort to see that he does understand at some time during his illness—he should be informed about the regulations of the hospital and why they have been made. The nurse can imply, although it would be unwise to state it baldly, that he may not be as ill as some of the patients in that same unit, but that the rules were made for the group, and that he must conform to them while he is a part of that particular group. The nurse must keep the patient aware of certain regulations, made for running a psychiatric hospital, but she can choose the terms she uses.

The hospitalized psychotic patient is not completely bereft of his senses. Unless he is in an acutely disturbed state, he may be approached the same as any other person; he deserves the same regard for his dignity. It is a temptation for the nurse in a psychiatric hospital to hold freedom before a patient as a sort of unreachable goal; unless he does one thing, he won't be permitted to go for a walk with the group; unless he stops doing another, she will tell the doctor who will not let the patient have visitors (how like a mother threatening to tell the policeman). The nurse should not use the truth—that the patient is confined behind locked doors—as a bludgeon. She can say that the patient appears too disturbed to get along well with the group today, that certain behavior is rude, that perhaps he better have a talk with the doctor before he sees visitors. Even such statements may turn out to be a threat to the disturbed patient, but they are not an affront to him.

We cannot always force the truth on patients; the nurse must learn to make concessions, but these should not be too threatening to herself. The psychotic or acutely neurotic and the very anxious patient often are in no condition to accept the truth about the immediate surroundings and happenings although they may beg the nurse to tell them. Often, we are unable to understand what disturbed patients mean by the truth. They may want you to confirm their fears or deny their fears, to protect them from reality or to define reality for them. The nurse needs to learn how to change a subject tactfully and still satisfy the patient; how to say frankly and without being defensive about it that she would rather not or cannot discuss the matter with the patient. She must then be prepared to offer him some other subject, absorbing enough for the patient to abandon his original request. The patient who keeps asking the nurse to assure him that "they are not waiting to kill me" is too sick to accept a flat denial or an explanation that "they" do not exist outside his mind. He can accept the nurse's firm and quiet, "You are perfectly safe here and I have some work for you to help me with." The first time such an approach is used may not be successful, but repeating it does help the patient to feel more secure.

Occasionally, a severely disturbed patient will hint at the truth in the midst of the wildest rambling, and the nurse can make use of that hint. I keep remembering the very psychotic young woman who stood in her room laughing aloud, flailing her arms, and slapping herself with a peculiar motion. I asked her what on earth she was doing, and she said, "I know it sounds crazy as hell, but my arms keep flying away from me and I have to catch them and put them on." I said, "It sure does sound crazy. Let's tear up some rags for a rug. That seems a little more useful." She laughed wildly, but agreeably began to work at tearing rags and became considerably calmer for a time. Often, we see acutely disturbed patients become calm when they observe that the nurse remains calm, asserts the truth quietly, and does not nag at them.

Telling psychotic patients the truth is quite different from repeating to them that certain facts are true. The nurse may have to say, "No, Mrs. Jones, your daughter is not dead. She came to see you yesterday at visiting hours, and she will be back again tomorrow," and repeat this in the same pleasant tone fifty times a day no matter how tiresome it is. The nurse must watch out that such repeating does not become nagging, such as, "you said you would eat today; you promised me you would eat your lunch; I thought you really meant it when you said you would eat." This can hardly be conducive to pleasant nurse-patient relationships. What annoys the well person is likely to annoy even more the emotionally disturbed person who is hypersensitive and easily upset.

The nurse must consider some other aspects of telling the truth. In the psychiatric hospital where nurses get to know patients intimately for long periods of time, there is a tendency to gossip with other personnel and with the "old timers" (patients who have been there for many months or even years.). A particular bit of gossip might be "true," and a patient may have picked it up and related it to the nurse; she should not confirm or deny it. She should suggest that this is pretty hurtful gossip and she would rather not indulge in it, nor would she want the patient to do so. Gossip will persist, but the nurse need not condone it nor take part in it, even if she wishes to set the gossip right by revealing the facts.

By and large, few persons are happy lying to someone or avoiding the truth, and few persons have learned to evade the truth skillfully. My own belief is that one should not do a job without having the skill for it; but each person must make up his own mind about what the truth is and how much of it to impart to patients.

Some nurses get a secondary pleasure from sharing the shock and distress of sick persons; some use the knowledge about patients as a weapon against them. There may be many reasons for this, but it is an administrative responsibility to see that such nurses are not in positions where they can hurt the patient. A nurse may be uneasy with the knowledge she has of details of a patient's private life. Her uneasiness may result in poorly disguised reactions to the patient's questions about his condition; it may make her abrupt or threatening. Certainly, this is not deliberate but part of a defense mechanism which operates in all of us. The administrator of a psychiatric hospital should be on the lookout for this type of reaction. The person reacting in this manner needs help and it should be offered. Being aware of the problem often helps the nurse avoid it. The professional person has a need for all the knowledge available, if he is to be really useful in helping the patient recover. The ability to handle such an uneasy burden of knowledge wisely is a sign of maturity, and we have every right to expect the professional person to be mature.

An important skill needed by the nurse who works with the mentally ill is her ability to size up a situation, meet it, and assume the responsibility for taking action; this involves telling the truth, but not always in so many words. I recall an incident in which the nurse never once mentioned the "truth" to the patient—that his mother was a nuisance but the nurse would protect him—and yet he recognized that the nurse knew the situation and was handling it to his benefit. The patient was a young man, an only child, almost "smothered" by his mother, and terribly confused about his feelings toward her. He had become so disturbed that hospitalization was urgent. His mother got him as far as the front door of the hospital when the lad balked. Several things could have been done. The nurse and aide who were sent to see how they could help made the quick decision to talk to the young man. They did so, quietly and cheerfully, but every time they thought they were making headway, the mother would break in to reassure her son that, "these nice people are trying to help you, Johnny," and all the good work seemed undone. After an hour of this, the nurse turned to the mother and said pleasantly and firmly, "I believe you may go now. John will come with us, and everything will be fine." The mother protested but allowed the nurse to lead her away. The effect on the patient was miraculous. He smiled, appeared relaxed, and offered the nurse a cigarette, which she accepted. The nurse, aide, and patient then sat on a bench outside the hospital door and talked for another hour. The nurse told him quietly that this was a locked hospital, that he would be in a locked ward, and explained a number of the hospital regulations. The young man took all this in gravely, and asked finally, "And if I don't come with you under my own power, you'll get help and carry me?" The nurse quietly said, "Yes," and sat back and waited. The patient got up, took the nurse's arm, turned to the aide, said, "Let's go," and walked into the hospital. He became a quiet and cooperative patient. Previously he had been in another hospital the reports of which stated that he had been taken there forcefully and had remained most disturbed and destructive.

It is not easy to tell the patient the truth. Indeed, not all of us can agree on what is the truth. But the nurse has an obligation to face facts honestly, and meet reality to the best of her ability. Certainly, she must use her judgment in many situations. The nurse who works in a mental hospital is called upon a little more frequently, I believe, than most nurses to look at a situation, weigh it, and reach a decision about her actions.

SHOULD THE PATIENT KNOW THE TRUTH?

Unconditionally Yes*

By Owen H. Wangensteen, M.D., Ph.D.

The most important person in an illness is the patient himself. Sometimes this is forgotten by the physician as well as relatives of the patient. Straightforward honesty and sincerity are traits which we appreciate in transactions with our fellow men and take for granted in our dealings with intimates. The physician-patient relationship is one which presumes trust, sincerity, faith, and confidence. And yet, how often we violate this trust when informing patients who have cancer concerning the nature of their illness. But why?

When Babe Ruth, hero of baseball, died in 1948, a well-known radio commentator said the nature of Ruth's illness had been so carefully hidden from him that he probably never knew he had cancer. One would have to be extremely gullible to believe that.

Yet, physicians frequently follow a policy of dissimulation in acquainting patients with the nature of a cancerous malady. We do not deliberately deceive the patient nor are we guilty of intentional fraud, but the deception is nevertheless a violation of that sincerity and trust which the patient rightfully may expect of his physician.

A critical examination of what we are accomplishing

* This is, in substance, the editorial "Should patients be told they have cancer?" that appeared in Surgery (27: 944, 1950) and is included here with permission of the journal.

by such artifice is very much in order. I have employed this stategy in earlier years in an attempt to evade informing patients who have cancer concerning the true nature of their illness. Although the word cancer may never have been spoken within the patient's hearing, I am convinced that the patient usually divines what we are striving to hide from him, particularly if the treatment carried out is only palliative. In fact, he too often becomes a party to the conspiracy, being careful not to let relatives or his physician learn that he (the patient) knows he has cancer.

What is the effect of such deception? In the first instance, it makes the patient mistrust his physician; moreover, it becomes difficult for him to understand the insincere behavior of his family. Many a patient, who has been caught up in this plot of deceit and has become fully aware that his strength is failing and nothing can be or is being done to help him, probably says to himself: "Why do not my physician and my relatives tell me the truth? Why do they lie and attempt to deceive me? They know very well what is the matter with me; they are blind if they do not perceive that I know and that I appreciate that they know. Why this atmosphere of faithless fraud? By their attempts at deception, my friends have destroyed what might have been a beautiful relationship in my final illness." In his loneliness the unhappy patient finds his only relief in bitterness, resentment, and self-pity.

Why do physicians and relatives conspire to try to hide from patients that they have cancer? Whatever the contributory causes may be, some of which will be mentioned presently, the real reason is undoubtedly an attempt to protect the patient from anxiety, fear, and worry, and to protect the family from needless uneasiness. We have already seen what this organized deception may do to the patient. For the family, life must go on, and anything done with a view to continuing a semblance of a normal mode of life is justified as being in the best interests of the patient. In other words, to tell the patient that he has cancer may upset the family routine, making it mandatory for the family and the patient to effect an adjustment in their relationship before it would otherwise have been necessary. The convenience of the family may very well be the issue finally and largely responsible for justifying the conspiracy against the patient. Leo Tolstoy depicts this situation in his story of "The Death of Ivan Ilich" written in 1886. Everyone, including the patient, knew he was dying; but his family, mindful of their own interests, affected to have Ivan believe that his illness was not serious.

Counterfeit behavior is not difficult to detect; even a sick man distinguishes easily in his associates the assumption of a light and Pollyannish air toward a matter which he knows intuitively is far more grave. Moreover, the very veering about in attitude of the relatives, from one of urging a concern on the part of the patient in his own illness to one of affected unconcern on their part, affirms in his mind the certainty of the seriousness of his disorder, whatever it may be.

It is not easy for anyone to share wholly the trials of another. History records no better example than that of Jesus with His disciples, Peter, James, and John, at Gethsemane. While the Master prayed for deliverance, they slept. Little wonder He was provoked to say: "The spirit indeed is willing, but the flesh is weak." These words have immortalized Gethsemane and made it a byword in our language.

The preceding lines were written years ago, directly

after hearing the radio commentator speak of Babe Ruth's illness. They relate essentially to the far-advanced case for whom the doctor can do little. How should the question be answered for the patient at an early stage of cancer? It is important to find out what patients think as well as what we do about this. In our hospital, the question was asked of patients in the Cancer Detection Center Group, of those who came to the outpatient clinic of the hospital, as well as of those who came because their home physicians believed or suspected they had cancer. The answer was plain: the majority of all these patients wanted to be dealt with sincerely and honestly. In other words, if, during the examination, cancer was discovered they expected and wanted to be told the truth.[1]

Yet, highly reputable surgeons fail to tell their patients they have cancer. From discussions with physicians and roentgenologists, as well as surgeons in several areas of this country, I infer that an evasive attitude is common practice. In McCall's Magazine for February, 1950, there was an article on this problem concerning breast cancer. It was a dialogue between a well-known American surgeon, Dr. Frank Adair of the Memorial Hospital in New York, and Mr. John Gunther. a modern writer of distinction, whose sensitive portrayal of his own son's illness in "Death Be Not Proud" touched the hearts of everyone who read it. Dr. Adair defended the thesis of not telling patients they have cancer and said that he never uses the word cancer at all.

To tell or not to tell the patient is of far greater import than mere differences in philosophic outlook. There is need, I believe, for a bolder and more realistic attitude, a more enlightened view toward cancer in dealing with our patients. In what other disease do we fail to acquaint patients with the nature of their illness? None that I know of. Is the discovery of cancer still synonymous with a sentence of doom? Certainly not, unless the cancer has been neglected. I have heard a prominent university professor in public health say, "Cancer may turn out to be a way of life." I do not feel that pessimistic over the outlook in cancer, nor do I believe there is any justification for such a belief.

Cancer is curable. Important progress in the treatment of cancer has been made during the past few years, essentially through combined and concerted efforts in stressing to the public the importance of early diagnosis. Whereas our main problem is early recognition, treatment of late cancer will probably always be with us, and we must continue to improve our management of the late case. In gastric, colic, or rectal cancer, a patient with symptoms has a cancer which is approximately twenty months old. If four months or more (an interval which is not unusual) intervene before the patient seeks treatment, the cancer has been developing for about two years by the time the patient reports for treatment. Hence it is of great importance to develop screening tests for cancer, and to have periodic careful examination of patients above 45 years of age when cancer begins to take a larger toll in both sexes. Will the time ever come when we will recognize the majority of the frequent cancers of the colon and rectum, stomach, breast, and uterus when these lesions are still local, without lymph node metastases? I do not know. I would like to think so. Certainly, if we continue to await the occurrence of symptoms, we shall continue dealing with late cancers—treating patients whose regional lymph nodes are involved, and in whom the cure rate, as contrasted with patients without lymph node involvement, drops from 75 to 20 per cent for the breast, colon, and rectum.

In the State of Connecticut, the five-year cure rate for all cancer was reported, in 1950, as being 33.5 per cent.[2] This is a record of substantial accomplishment. It sets a high standard for states with a less crystallized program and interest in cancer. And yet that record too, I believe, will be improved upon.

The majority of patients with cancers upon whom we operate have lymph node metastases (approximately 75 per cent). As regards patients with colon, rectal, and stomach cancers with lymph node involvement, my colleagues and I have come to the point of view that such patients should undergo reoperation for a "second look" within four to six months.[3] In the visceral cancers treated in this manner, 75 per cent have been found to have cancer at the time of the "second look." In a few patients, we have done another and still another "second look." Our objective in such patients is one "second look" in which no cancer is found. Operative results for cancer of the colon, thus far,[4] have shown that we are salvaging approximately 30 per cent of those patients who are still lymph node positive on the occasion of the first "second look" and who presumably would die in a few months or, at most, a year or two ahead.

Obviously, it would be absurd to fail to tell the patient he has cancer. If we want the patient's cooperation which we must have, of necessity, he must be told. A well-known judge in my community came to talk with me about his operation a few weeks after leaving the hospital. He said, "Did I have cancer?" My answer was in the affirmative. I then countered by saying, "When did you first learn?" He said, "I looked at the chart." We are all being examined every day, perhaps not by judges of the law but by persons whose clarity and acuity of vision in this important matter transcends our own. To fail to tell patients they have cancer is as archaic and outmoded as Victorianism.

REFERENCES

1. Kelly, W. D., and Friesen, S. R.: Do cancer patients want to be told? Surgery *27*:822, 1950.
2. Dublin, L. I.: Recent progress in cancer control. Statistical Bulletin, Metropolitan Life Insurance Co. *30*: No. 3, 1950.
3. Wangensteen, O. H.: Cancer of the colon and rectum. Wisconsin M. J. *48*:591, 1949.
4. Wangensteen, O. H., Lewis, J., and others: An interim report upon the "second look" procedure for cancer of the stomach, colon, and rectum, etc. Surg., Gynec. & Obst. *99*:257, 1954.

In a Cancer Hospital

By Edith S. Wolf, R.N., A.M.

In cancer nursing our question is whether or not the definite diagnosis of cancer should be made known to the patient.

For many years it has been a custom in this country to think of heart disease, the number one killer in our society, as an honorable affliction. Cancer, the number two killer, is spoken of in hushed tones and with bated breath. This attitude is not confined to lay persons but also pervades professional groups, physicians and nurses included.

One of the most potent factors in caring for the patient with cancer is the attitude of the nurse toward the disease itself. I know that nurses who work specifically with cancer are asked very often: "How can you do it? It must be depressing." Of course, this judgement is formed by individuals who know very little about cancer or its modern treatment.

One of the ways in which a nurse can develop a hopeful attitude toward cancer is by getting informed on all aspects of the disease and its treatment. Ignorance and delay are cancer's best friends. Early diagnosis and effective treatment cure many cancers. Treatment of cancer is ever aggressive, and trends and approaches are constantly being revised and perfected. Both patient and nurse can be cheerful and hopeful that tomorrow may bring the answer to the cause and cure of this disease—when we can say "cure rate" instead of "survival rate."

The nurse needs a sound understanding of the why and wherefore of radical surgery. Many doctors and nurses stress that the patient is not cured by these radical procedures. This is true, but the patient has been greatly helped in at least three ways:

1. A tumor has been removed and, therefore, cannot become a fungating, foul-smelling, sloughing growth which makes life unbearable for the patient and those around him.

2. With the tumor removed the patient has little or no pain. He is much more comfortable, and the need for hypnotic drugs is eliminated. This is especially important because of the many problems involved when hypnotics are used over long periods of time and in large amounts. Addiction, mental deterioration, and cost of the drug are problems that readily come to mind.

3. Psychological care of patients with cancer is important. To reassure a depressed or fearful patient, the nurse must be tactful and understanding without being untruthful or unreasonably optimistic. The patient is exposed to two major threats, the disease and surgery which often is extensive and mutilating. Reassurance by the nurse is not enough to help these patients. The nurse must be well versed in teaching them to care for themselves, thus starting their rehabilitation early.

Individuals react in various ways to problems. When a person who has always blocked out his every-day problems becomes ill, it is unlikely that he will admit to symptoms or any discussion about them. On the other hand, there are individuals who spend a great deal of time in clinics and doctors' offices complaining of many symptoms, some organic and others psychosomatic. Fear, however, appears to be the basic factor, operating in both types.

Few can expect to escape being involved with cancer, either personally or as a friend or relative. It is, therefore, not only doctors and nurses who are faced with the problem of telling the patient with cancer the truth but also many responsible members of the patient's family.

I believe, the majority of patients do not wish to know the truth. The truth about someone else, yes; but in their own case, no. When a patient enters an institution that treats only cancer, then, surely he must have some awareness that he personally is involved with the disease. In my experience, working with doctors, the word cancer has never been used. The patient is told he has a tumor or growth that needs treatment. This appears to satisfy many patients. Dr. James Mackenzie once wrote that practically every patient who consulted him wanted to know not what ailed him but what was to be the outcome of his complaint. However, when a patient says to the nurse, "Do I have cancer?" the nurse simply asks, "Do you think you have cancer?" Usually the conversation changes to something else and no more mention is made of cancer, the patient apparently being unwilling to commit himself to what he believes regarding his condition. If a patient persists, he is gently but firmly told, as in any other diagnosis, that he must ask his doctor for further information.

Recently, in leafing through a magazine my attention was drawn to a picture of a young woman with an expression of terror and horror on her face. A man's back in the picture shows that she is facing him. The man is a husband telling his young pregnant wife, that by the time their baby is born she will be dying of leukemia. The only thoughts in my mind were the words: "Vengeance is mine, I will repay saith The Lord." (Romans XII, 19)

"Should the patient know the truth?" is and will continue to be a controversial question. We all know of people with long-term illnesses who have faced indescribable pain and suffering with spiritual courage, some knowing their diagnosis, but most of them seemingly unaware of it. The nurse, as a professional person, will follow the orders and pattern set by the doctors with whom she works. I am sure that all doctors, regardless of their approach, agree that a responsible member of the family must be told.

BIBLIOGRAPHY

ABRAMS, R. D., AND FINESINGER, J. E.: Guilt reactions in patients with cancer. Cancer *6*:474, 1953.

CAMERON, C. S.: Professional attitudes and terminal care. Public Health Report *67*:955, 1952.

KNAPP, F.: How do you feel about cancer? Nursing Outlook *2*:350, 1954.

ORBACH, C. E., AND SUTHERLAND, A. M.: In Depression, edited by P. H. Hoch and J. Zubin. New York, Grune & Stratton, 1954.

SOLOMON, H.: Psychiatric implications of cancer. Rocky Mountain M. J. *44*:801, 1947.

SUTHERLAND, A. M.: Psychological impact of cancer surgery. Cancer *5*:857, 1952.

A Surgeon's Kindness Comes Through

By Henry W. Cave, M.D.

Any physician who undertakes the care of a patient suffering from cancer or another incurable disease must search his soul before he can do what is best for the patient. The problem requires intelligence, conscientiousness, and courage.

It has been my feeling that most cancer patients do not want to know the truth. Without question, many of these people whom you tell that they have not a cancer instinctively know that they have. This may be because of the lack of conviction with which the doctor handles the situation.

Most surgeons would much rather tell the truth to most of their patients but they cringe from telling the truth about cancer. They feel that informing a responsible member of the family about the exact nature and hopelessness of the case is all that needs to be done. When the patients are elderly, it seems to me that deception is in order, unless there is a definite reason for them to know the truth. Business and financial affairs play a part when the surgeon is told or knows that important decisions must be made by a hopelessly sick patient.

In the majority of instances, I am not in favor of telling the patient the truth. Yet, when I do not tell the truth, I have a severe pang and say to myself: "I am deceiving. Why do I do this?" I do it because it is mostly the best thing for the patient not to know or not to have his fears confirmed. Several experiences I had will show how difficult it may be to cope with the truth.

About fourteen years ago, a woman and her husband came to my office. She said briskly, immediately upon coming into the consultation room: "Doctor, I have a tumor in my breast. I want to let you understand that I wear the pants in this family and I must know the whole truth." Her poor husband agreed. After I had examined her carefully, she asked me, "Is that a cancer or not?" I told her that I could not say definitely, but that it appeared to me to be a cancer. She then asked when I was going to operate on her, and I answered it would be as soon as I could get her on the schedule. After the operation she asked me again if she had a cancer and I said "yes." She stayed around New York for two years and I examined her every three months during that time. She then moved to California. Ten years later she came back to New York and wanted to be examined for recurrence. There was no evidence of recurrence. When I assured her of this she turned to me and said: "Why did you tell me the truth? I have suffered every day through all these years wondering whether I had a recurrence. You should not have told me the truth, Doctor!" Although this woman had insisted on getting the facts, she felt I deserved severe criticism.

Another experience, some ten years ago, shows how embarrassing the results of deception can become. I did a radical operation for cancer of the breast. The patient's husband demanded that I did not tell her the truth. Obviously, I had to resort to bold deception and stick to it. Such a demand and course of action takes it out of any person. Several years after the operation, the woman came to my office and asked me point blank whether or not the tumor that I had removed had been benign or malignant. When I reassured her that it had been a benign tumor, she accused me of lying to her. She said she knew the truth from her husband. He had, in fact, broken down and told her. I then was frank and explained that her husband demanded that I did not tell her the truth but that he had used poor judgment.

It is much easier for the surgeon when he tells the truth and does not have to burden his soul with a deep sense of deception. Many years ago, when I was an assistant to a fine surgeon here in New York, I assisted him in an operation on a man 74 years of age for acute mesenteric thrombosis. On exploration, almost the entire small bowel was found to be gangrenous. Nothing constructive could be done. My chief went to Chicago the next day. When I walked into the patient's room in the morning, he asked me, "Am I going to get well." I said, "Of course, you are going to get well." His wife saw me outside the room and said that I had to tell him the whole truth. When I came back into his room the next time and he asked whether I was sure he was going to get well, I told him that he would not survive. He wanted to know how long he would live; I told him about two or three days. He said to me: "Doctor, I am a religious man and I want to get a minister up here and a choir and I want to have a sermon preached to me." This was carried out and the man died peaceful.

It is an important and a frightfully difficult part of surgical work to know what to do for the patient. There are many patients who ask me prior to operation: "Doctor, do you think this is malignant?" I say to them that I cannot tell for sure, that frozen section or paraffin section will tell the tale. It is pitiful, too, to see some patients who think they want to know the truth, but in reality do not want to know it. I am convinced that not to know the truth will cause the least mental anguish to many patients and that a surgeon may have to carry out deception, no matter how distasteful this may be to him.

Ultimately, each surgeon must draw on his own professional experience and his own resources as a human being. For myself I have come to the conclusion that each patient and each situation is an individual one and must be seen and handled as such. When the prognosis leaves very little hope for the patient, generally he does not want to know that his disease is a potential and likely killer. I am convinced this is true for most people. It is, however, the duty of the surgeon to acquaint the next of kin or responsible member of the family with the facts as they are.

Other Times, Other Fears

By Isidore Snapper, M.D.

There are many instances when the patient should not be told that he is suffering from a very serious, possibly incurable disease. In such cases, one of the family members should be informed. On the other hand, I remember the times when no physician ever told his patient that he had tuberculosis because it was thought that this information would undermine the patient's confidence in recovery. I have an open mind whether in the field of cancer an evolution is taking place comparable to the one that happened in the field of tuberculosis. Maybe that the younger generation of patients has lost its fear of cancer and will in the future be able to bear the truth about this disease.

What One Neurosurgeon Does

By Leo M. Davidoff, M.D.

Almost every good doctor realizes that, but for the grace of God, he might be sitting or lying in the patient's place, himself a patient, entrusting his health and very existence to another physician. With this picture constantly and vividly in his mind, the doctor will endeavor to treat any patient before him as he himself would like to be treated if he should be in the patient's place. Good doctors, however, are all kinds of good people, and there can be no rule for answering the question, "Should the patient be told?" Among physicians there are many who, if they were the patient, would rather not be told; yet, in my estimation, the majority of our profession would prefer to know the truth. Since I belong to the latter group, my viewpoint is biased, naturally, in this direction. On the other hand, thirty-five years of experience with patients, and the families of patients, suffering from serious and often fatal disease have taught me that in human relationships the adage, "One man's meat is another man's poison," is nowhere more applicable than to this situation.

What a patient should be told depends on the patient's personality. The personality make-up of the patient may be misjudged by the physician. To complicate matters, the patient's nearest of kin may insist on modifying what the physician may be convinced is the proper thing to tell the patient.

My experience has led me to the firm opinion that the patients who want to know will either ask the physician questions so directly that no evasive answer is possible, or make it their business to find out from some other source. The patients who should not be told that they are suffering from a malignant disease are, in effect, those who do not wish to be told. Perhaps the best rules to follow are: not to offer any voluntary opinions and to make the answers fit the patient's questions. This, I am sure, can be done without lying, in the way one answers a child when he becomes curious about sex.

A patient, unwilling to face the issue, may be pathetically naive in his attempt to fool himself. I have seen a neurologist who could not have failed to make the diagnosis of a malignant tumor of the brain, if he had evaluated his own history like that of another patient. He made himself believe that he had had a mild "stroke." After being operated upon (which he "knew" is practically never done for a stroke), he insisted that a small blood clot had been removed; he finally came to believe that this was what the neurosurgeon had told him. In contrast, another neurologist who developed symptoms of a malignant brain tumor made the correct diagnosis on himself and was in terror lest he lose his power of reasoning before he could convince me that he chose not to be operated upon; I reassured him that I wouldn't.

Another equally important side of the problem is *how* the patient should be told. In this sphere we face a serious matter of semantics. Take, for example, the words malignant and benign. Few lay people have heard "benign" applied to a tumor. When the surgeon attempts to define the term by using the word "good" in connection with it (the German word is actually *gutartig,* that is good-natured) the patient and his family are puzzled because in their estimation *no* tumor can be good or good-natured. To the pathologist, "malignant" means every tumor that is not benign, though the malignancy may vary in degree from something that, for all intents and purposes, is a curable lesion to a fulminating type that can carry a patient from seemingly complete health to his death within less than a week. To most lay people, however, the word malignant is synonymous with cancer, and cancer is bad. Yet the surgeon must be prepared, after telling the family or the patient himself that a tumor was found, to answer the frequent query, "Was it malignant, Doctor?" Unless it is a benign tumor, it would be malignant, by the pathologist's definition; yet to answer "Yes" to the question, except for a truly cancerous malignant growth, is as misleading as if one had deliberately and maliciously lied.

In my own practice, which to a very large degree deals with all kinds of tumors of the brain, I handle the problem as follows. As soon after the operation as possible, I make it a point to see the nearest relatives of the patient. If a benign tumor was found and removed, and the patient withstood the procedure well, my first words are, "I have good news for you." I go on to tell that a tumor was found and removed; that its nature is such that it was completely separate from brain tissue; that it was removed together with its own sac or membrane or capsule; that the patient has withstood the procedure well; that there is every reason to expect an uncomplicated recovery and a cure of the disease, and no reason to anticipate its recurrence. As soon as the patient has sufficiently recovered from the anesthetic, the good news may be told him as well.

If the patient has a very malignant tumor, I tell the relatives that a tumor was found and removed, and that the patient has withstood the procedure well. Mostly, the relatives will then immediately ask, "Was it malignant, Doctor?" My answer is, that it was a growth within the brain substance itself, and that the separation of brain tissue from tumor was not too clearly defined; that we tried to stay well beyond the area of brain grossly involved by tumor; that under the circumstances it may have been completely removed though with some sacrifice of brain tissue; that, however, the final judgment as to prognosis cannot be made until after a report by the laboratory which may take four or five days. When the laboratory report arrives and perchance bears out the most optimistic interpretation of the gross findings, this can be transmitted joyously to the family and even to the patient. If the growth proves to be really malignant, some responsible member of the family must be told. Whether the patient is told or not will then depend on what he wants to know. The questions and answers may be something like this:

Paticnt: "Well, Doctor, how did it go?'

Doctor: "Fine, fine, everything went very well."

Patient: "Was everything removed that doesn't belong there?"

Doctor: "Yes, it's all out."

Patient: "Thank you, Doctor."

The interview frequently ends here. If the patient, by further questions, insists on knowing the truth, it must be told to him in such a way and with the choice of such words, that the patient can face the facts as they exist.

The doctor must explain fully and cannot leave any interpretation of terms to the patient. It is often helpful to draw a diagram while explaining. This is a grave and important moment in the life of the patient, and the physician must treat it with the seriousness it deserves.

I believe that the patient should be told what he wants to be told; and what he wants to be told becomes apparent to the perceptive doctor in the patient's manner of asking for information.

An Obstetrician Meets Adversities

By Alan F. Guttmacher, M.D.

Many problems in this sphere confronting the obstetrician and gynecologist are not unique to his specialty. These non-specific problems are being presented by other contributors and therefore this discussion will be limited to topics confined to the field of obstetrics and gynecology.

Infertility. The couple unable to achieve pregnancy eventually find their way to the specialist. He puts both through a battery of tests. There may be no abnormal findings and in this event the truth is pleasant to reveal. However, in most cases one of the marital partners is either relatively infertile or perhaps even sterile. If therapy is possible, the doctor frankly assesses the situation and makes his recommendations, at the same time warning against charlatans who may promise a more certain and dramatic result. On the other hand, if either the husband or wife is irrevocably sterile, the physician has to determine what he will tell, first, to the individual, and, then, to his marital partner.

At the Johns Hopkins, when I was a student, we had a remarkably sensitive and excellent professor of medicine, Dr. William Sidney Thayer, who lectured our fourth-year class on what the doctor should tell the patient. I remember vividly his succinct remark: "The doctor is never privileged to lie to a patient, but he is privileged to tell the patient part of the truth."

Believing in this philosophy, when I find either partner absolutely sterile, I will talk with him or her frankly. However, I rarely state the truth in bald terms, that is, "You can never have a baby." I simply say that tests show that it is tremendously doubtful that either he or she will be a parent, suggesting that they bend their thinking toward adoption or some other means of meeting the problem. I then ask the wife, if she is the one in whom I have localized the fault, whether or not the situation should be revealed to the husband. Or, if sterility is found to be the husband's fault, I ask whether or not the wife should be told. Getting the advice and permission of the marital partner is important, because if the marriage is a fragile one such tragic news by the physician might tear it asunder. In most instances the patient will say, "I wish you to tell my wife or husband exactly what you told me; we've always shared our problems." On the other hand, particularly when the husband is at fault, he may wish the physician to minimize the problem as much as possible to the wife.

There should be a clear-cut and precise statement to one or the other. Unless the doctor tells the truth, the couple will continue to go from specialist to specialist, wasting funds and building up hopes anew each time they hear of some infertile couple being aided by this or that doctor.

Fetal death before labor. There are some problems in what to tell the patient which are strictly confined to obstetrics; these concern the plight of the fetus or newborn. Unfortunately for obstetrician as well as patient, it is not unusual for a fetus to die in utero. Frequently the patient comes to the physician and, not appreciating the gravity of the situation, says casually, "It's very odd doctor, but I haven't felt my baby move for two or three days." With such a history, when auscultation for the fetal heart is negative and palpation of the abdomen elicits no fetal movements, the doctor can almost be certain that death of the fetus has occurred; this can be assumed, if pregnancy has progressed to the 30th week when the fetal heart is usually easy to auscultate and movements simple to elicit. Earlier in pregnancy there may be serious room for doubt; the patient may fail to appreciate fetal movements for a day or two, without it being truly significant.

When clinical evidence bespeaks fetal death, it is my policy to tell the patient I fear there is bad news, that the absence of fetal movements and the findings make it almost certain that the baby has died in utero. However, under some circumstances and with some patients I may qualify my remarks by saying, it is perfectly possible there may be an error, and, if so, in the next day or two there might be a change in the whole picture. With the intelligent and emotionally stable patient this kind of amelioration of the situation is not necessary. A patient with an intra-uterine death almost always asks about the next step. The doctor has to reassure her that the presence of a dead fetus in the uterus in no way jeopardizes her health and that it is best to await the spontaneous onset of labor. He must caution her that patients may go days or even weeks after fetal death before labor begins. If labor can be easily and safely induced, it is humane to do it.

In addition to the patient, the family poses a problem. The husband will want some explanation if one exists; much pressure will be brought to bear on the doctor by even distant relatives and friends to terminate the pregnancy. It takes character on the part of the doctor to turn a deaf but sympathetic ear to the well-meaning advice of these poorly informed advisers.

Diagnosis of abnormal fetus before its birth. A somewhat similar problem faces the obstetrician when he diagnoses a grossly abnormal fetus still living and still in utero. Sometimes, the diagnosis is made weeks or months before the expected term date. The lesion, usually anencephaly, occasionally hydrocephaly, is found in an x-ray picture, taken because of an associated hydramnios or bizarre findings on palpation.

Since I find it the best policy to deal frankly with patients and to treat them as mature individuals, I tell the husband the exact truth and ask advice and permission to tell the wife that things are not normal with the baby and that she should not anticipate a good result. It is cruel to allow a woman to continue pregnant, finally go into labor expecting a normal baby, and then find the truth. When the diagnosis is made, we usually attempt to induce labor so that the patient will not have to remain pregnant for a useless number of additional weeks. Labor cannot always be induced, but, as soon as it can, it is certainly wise to do it.

The breaking of bad news. Another problem which faces the obstetrician is what to tell the pregnant woman when some catastrophe has happened in her family, such as the death of a near relative. Most of us who practiced during the last war had to break the news of the death of a soldier-husband to a pregnant wife. Once, I had to tell this news to a young woman who had given birth but 24 hours before to her second child. The husband had been killed in an airplane crash in Texas and the General of his Air Force Command got in touch with me and asked that I handle the terrible news as I thought best. The patient's uncle, her nearest relative, was a distinguished judge. I called to ask him to help me, but the judge was so overwhelmed that he had to go to bed. I went to the hospital, ordered a quarter of morphine for the patient, and about 15 minutes later went to her room and said, as gently as I could, that I had some bad news. The patient sensed the truth and asked me immediately whether the news was the death of her aviator husband. I told her so at once.

As far as I know, telling a pregnant woman or a recently delivered woman tragic news, if done in the proper way, does not have worse results than telling her if she was not pregnant or puerperal. Abortion, hemorrhage, and other untoward sequelae do not result.

On a few occasions, I have withheld bad news from a patient. In almost every instance the news reached the patient in some shocking manner. It would have been far better if either the husband or I had told her at once.

Birth of a living malformed infant. Finally, we must consider what to tell parents about a malformed child. If it is a lethal malformation, recovery from which is impossible, I prevent the mother from seeing the new baby and within a few hours after birth tell her that the child is feeble, has a poor prognosis, and probably will not survive. It makes a horrible and indelible impression upon a mother to tell her that her baby is malformed, and nothing is gained by the telling. I attempt to dissuade the father from seeing such a baby, but tell in some detail of its anatomical distortions. If he insists, I show it to him. When such a baby dies, we plead that the body be given to the state for autopsy and disposal.

Then, there is the abnormal newborn who is fated to

survive. If there is a correctable skeletal abnormality, like a hare lip, a cleft palate, or club feet, it is wise to get the appropriate consultant to see the child before discussing the problem with the family. In the presence of the husband, I bring in the surgical consultant, sometimes the pediatrician; the group of medical advisers discusses the whole problem as frankly as possible with the parents and perhaps the grandparents, painting as optimistic a picture as truth will allow. The greatest curse for the mother and the obstetrician is the news that her child is a Mongolian idiot. The patient is unlikely to make such a diagnosis herself, and it comes to her and her husband as a tremendous shock. Since nothing can be done about mongolism the first several weeks, we usually wait that long before gradually breaking this terrible news. The obstetrician and pediatrician may want to handle the problem together and they have to be prepared to give parents advice about (1) what to do with the child and (2) and what the possibility is of normal subsequent offspring.

Unexpected stillbirth. When delivery results in unanticipated stillbirth, I usually delay until six or eight hours after delivery and then go into the room alone, sit on the side of the bed and tell the patient that I have unhappy news, gradually revealing the fact that her child was stillborn. I usually follow this by a discussion of the cause and immediately begin talking about the future; if one can assure a patient that the cause of the stillbirth is not likely to be repetitive, hope for the future numbs the unhappiness of the present. During the same visit, I tell the patient that it is my policy to advise reimpregnation as soon as the six-week recuperative period has elapsed. The more promptly the patient again achieves pregnancy, the less deep will be the wound from the recent, unhappy event.

These are the problems which are more or less specific to the specialty of the obstetrician-gynecologist. My philosophy is to be quite frank with patients, telling them the truth; sometimes part of the truth, but usually the whole truth. Often it is not precisely what the doctor says, but how he says it which makes the unhappy truth bearable, or, at least, palatable.

The Sick Child Knows

By Ruth Frank Baer, R.N., M.N.

What are children like in a terminal illness? I have taken care of many of them. I believe I can recall most of them vividly. Not that they were all vivid personalities. On the contrary, children who are that ill seem to withdraw unto themselves. The fight, panic, and anxiety that one is accustomed to see in adults is rarely found in a child. A very sick child is usually quiet, apathetic. He may be irritable, unhappy with pain and discomfort, but he seems to find peace and solace in escape from the immediate world around him.

I remember Ronny. He was only two. He would lie in his bed, on his side, head turned toward the wall, eyelids lowered. When you approached his bed he would turn his head even further away. His whole posture seemed to say, "Leave me alone. Don't make me move, don't make me hurt anymore. I'm all right this way."

Terry who was two and a half would stand at the end of his crib, his pale little face propped on his hands, his wide eyes surveying the ward. When I approached his bed he would make no sign of recognition until I let down the cribsides. He then would murmur "mama, mama" and stretch out his arms. All he wanted was to be held in my lap. He would sit quietly as long as I would hold him. When placed back in bed, he would whimper and turn away. Danny, age three, in the next bed was getting well. "Dat's not your mamma," he would say and want a toy. Jackie was five and was failing rapidly during Christmas. He showed no excitement over the tree in his room, over Santa Claus' visit, or his new toys. He would sit quietly in his bed and finger his old toys. One day I came in to find him carefully tearing apart a new toy bunny, muttering under his breath, "Damn Santy Claus, damn Santy Claus," but his tone was one of resignation, defeat.

Obviously, we do not tell these children they are not going to get well. Even if we did, we would be foolish to think they understand the way we do. We do not tell children if it is hopeless, but we do tell the parents; at least, the doctor does. The nurse has an easier role. She does not have to make the decision as to what and when to tell the parents. But she does go along with the doctor and she is often the one who feels the brunt of the parents' emotions.

I have often wondered, but never asked what it is that makes the doctor decide when to tell the parents. Would the same doctor tell the same parent if the parent was the patient and had a terminal cancer? Does the doctor believe that parents can manage the truth about their children more easily than they can about themselves? I have an impression that parents are told the truth about their child's illness almost as soon as the doctor knows himself. And often I have wished that the parents had not known so soon.

What happens when a parent learns the truth about his sick or abnormal or dying child? There are a few rare people who, as parents, can accept misfortune and deal with it with equilibrium. Some parents of severely retarded children, for example, can accept the facts and the doctor's recommendations. But there are others who cannot accept the truth, who deny the evidence before their eyes, who go from doctor to doctor, from hospital to hospital, in the hope that all the doctors they have seen have been wrong. These are the parents who, on seeing their child paler and thinner, will say brightly to the nurse, "His color is so much better today." And the nurse, who wants that child to get well, remains silent.

What does the child know of the truth? Children, especially sick ones, are remarkably perceptive. They seem to have an uncanny knack of sizing up a situation. One does not have to tell them. I recall a child on an open ward who suddenly died in his sleep. He was quickly wheeled in his bed into the closed treatment room, a not unusual procedure on this particular ward. Then we nurses carefully told the other children that Johnny had been transferred to another part of the hospital. Later that day, I heard one of the children tell another, "Johnny died, but don't tell the nurses."

Children appear to know. Bob who had hemophilia was told he could get very sick if he got into a fight and received a severe bruise or cut, but he was not told that such a condition might be fatal. But Bob knew. On one occasion he was admitted to the hospital after playing football with a neighborhood gang. He was quite resigned to his condition which was grave and told me that he did not want to live unless he could be like other guys.

The concepts of younger children are quite different, and they cannot put them in words; yet they too seem to accept the fact of their illness. If solid foods do not stay down, they do not ask for those foods just because the other children have them. They are content with liquids. A mother, denying even to herself that her child is failing, tries to persuade him to eat a piece of bread and butter or a cookie. And the nurse too, always hoping that this particular child will get better, encourages him to eat something else. Nurse and mother are fighting for the child to get well, while the child seems to have accepted the fact that he will not.

What of the children whose prognosis is good? What about the truth then? Do we tell a child he is going to have an operation? That he will have a cast on his leg? Yes, we do. We have found that children have a great ability to tolerate pain and discomfort if it is predictable for them. A child's fear is of the unknown, of his own fantasy. If we can help him to manage reality, if we can reassure him that his mother or another adult will be there to help him, he can rise to most any occasion. We say: "When you wake up your tummy will hurt and you will feel bad, but soon you will feel good again. And I'll be right here with you." A child who understands this has much easier post-operative hours than the child who wakes bewildered and frightened, not knowing what to expect.

We tell the child with a rheumatic heart that he will be sick if he runs too much or plays football, and we help him to accept his limitations by showing him all the things he can do.

The child with a severe emotional problem is also told the truth. Not bluntly, of course. The long-term aim of treatment for such a child is for the child to learn the truth about himself and manage that truth. This learning may be largely an emotional one. To get better, the child must learn to manage his own shortcomings of personality; he must recognize what his emotions are, what makes them go out of control and what keeps them under control. In this way, he begins to cope with his problem. We do not usually tell the parents the truth about their emotionally disturbed children, not the whole truth. Few parents of such children are able to manage the truth. Could you tell the parent of the disturbed child that the child hates him? Not if you want that parent and child to get along together in the future. Half-truths or inferences can often be used. Also, the parents are helped in managing their own emotions so that they get along better with their child.

I believe parents want to hear the truth about their sick child. They may not accept it when told, but they would become angry with any doctor who lied to them or withheld information. As a parent I feel strongly about this, though I am not so sure I would always want to know the truth about myself. If I know the truth about my child, I can do what I believe is best. Children are so dependent and have so many needs we can satisfy, that we feel tremendous responsibility toward them. Perhaps it is this fact that makes me feel the truth is so important where my child is concerned.

To a nurse caring for another's child, the other very different side of the coin presents itself. I have often felt that it is not fair or right for any mother to know her child has leukemia. Why must she know for so long a time that her child will die? Why must she mourn the child with each exacerbation and have false hopes with each remission?

A nurse when caring for a seriously ill child must be

ready for a special problem. The parents, frantic, anxious, sometimes guilt-ridden, may blame the nurse when the child is not comfortable or takes a turn for the worse. They may project their own fears and their own anxiety on the nurse and her work. In such cases it takes great patience and understanding for the nurse to continue her work calmly and skillfully. If she is tired, if she is not mature emotionally, she may find herself in an unfortunate situation.. A nurse is expected to give skilled care to the children as well as understanding and guidance to the parents. When the parents are not able to manage the emotional stress of the situation, it places an added burden on the nurse, sometimes one with which she is unable to cope. Can the nurse point out the truth, the facts, to the parents? She can, by refering them to the doctor.

Some parents feel that nurses have become hardened to suffering and death. Perhaps they have, for it would pull each one apart if she became as attached to her patients as their parents are. A nurse becomes attached to her patients in her own way, and often a child has a special meaning for her. Once, I kept asking a doctor for months, whether Kathy had come into the clinic for a check-up. She had been taken off the ward by her parents when they learned she had not long to live. Intellectually I knew Kathy must have passed on, but I wanted to see her again.

In pediatrics, we tell the patient the truth when we can do so constructively. If a child is going to get better, and we can help him do so, we tell him in simple terms what is going to happen so that he can understand and manage the situation. But when there is little that we can do to help, we deny the truth. We do not tell, but somehow children seem to know, like Jerry, age eight, who would look at you wisely and say, "Soon I'm going to fly right out of here." And we, not wanting to accept the truth ourselves, think Jerry has been reading Superman too much. No, we do not tell the truth, for with children it is difficult to manage it ourselves.

A Cardiac Consultant's Way

By Paul D. White, M.D.

My contribution to the discussion of the question "Should the Patient Know the Truth" can be briefly presented. It is based on several features of my personal experience with cardiac patients seen in private practice and in the wards and Out Patient Department of the Massachusetts General Hospital during the past thirty-five years.

In the first place, what is the truth? Are we always sure of the diagnosis and, even if we are, can we state with certainty what the prognosis is? We can rarely be dogmatic. I have seen harm come from attempts so to be. A former instructor of mine, years ago, used to tell patients not only what he thought was wrong with them but also what he thought would happen to them; he stated this dogmatically and very briefly, disregarding the fact that he could not prophesy with certainty. When I was serving my medical internship in the hospital I had the occasion not infrequently to console patients in the wards to whom he had painted too dark a picture. Usually the course which the disease of these patients later took did not fit the picture that he painted. In his vigorous effort to be truthful he proved to be at times quite untruthful.

The next point I want to bring out is that, despite the difficulty mentioned in the last paragraph, in fact because of it, I have found that with most patients it is very valuable to have a full and often a lengthy discussion of what we know and what we don't know of their illness. The time spent in the presentation, even of the details, is very important for the understanding of the patient, in obtaining his cooperation, and in the future treatment and follow-up. Almost all patients are intelligent enough to take part in such a discussion. Their fears are usually dispelled. It is the fear of the unknown and of brief mysterious statements and prognostications that does the greatest harm. Most individuals know when they are very ill and they don't usually ask the doctor at such a time what their exact status is or just how long they are going to live, even if the doctor should happen to know. In such a discussion, naturally, tact and kindness are of great importance.

The third feature of my experience in dealing with cardiac patients has been to recognize and, in most instances, to help the patient himself to recognize that heart disease is not just one disease and of one degree of severity. There are all kinds of heart disease and all degrees of seriousness. There is actually such a condition as a "touch" of heart disease. Also, many times the patient is bothered by multiple symptoms referred to the heart that are not due to heart disease at all.

A very important point is the proper definition of a "heart attack." For most laymen a heart attack sounds serious and ominous, whereas doctors know that there are various kinds of heart attacks, many of them quite harmless. Even for a coronary heart attack there are all degrees of severity and of recovery from the attack. In my own experience, I have seen patients with coronary heart attacks, that is, coronary thrombosis of moderate severity, who recovered completely and have been well for many years afterwards, living active and healthy lives ten, twenty, or twenty-five years after an attack, even with scars in their hearts. Of course, this is not true of all cases. Some individuals may die quickly in a heart attack; most patients, however, recover. Very often, recovery is so complete that one would not suspect that there had ever been any such past history.

The fourth feature of my experience is that in nearly every case one can give help even if not a cure. Life is sweet for most persons and not easily given up. If a cure cannot be effected, tolerable comfort can usually be maintained, sometimes for years, even in the presence of serious heart disease.

The fifth point concerns patients who are seriously ill with what seems to be an incurable and crippling condition. It is often very helpful to point out the importance of medical research now constantly and increasingly in progress; that there are new discoveries every year "right around the corner" which may turn the tide in the treatment of the disease the particular patient is suffering from. Two practical applications of this can be mentioned:

1. The introduction of the marvelous cardiovascular surgery of the day; these operations have prolonged the lives of innumerable patients, considered until recently the victims of chronic and hopeless disease of the heart valves or of congenital defects.

2. The utilization of radioactive iodine in easing the symptoms and prolonging the lives, sometimes for years, of patients chronically and seriously incapacitated by either coronary insufficiency or heart muscle failure.

Finally, it has been my experience through the years and increasingly so that to instil optimism and a cheerful outlook on physical ills is very helpful both in treatment and in prognosis. The raising of the morale has a favorable physiological effect in itself and, I am certain, tends to counteract some of the harmfulness resulting from the so-called alarm reaction. A cheerful outlook is often fully justified if added to the medical or surgical measures that are being carried out, and it may be the one additional factor that turns the tide and wins the battle.

The personal experience that I have presented applies especially to cardiac patients but a good deal of it may, I am quite sure, be helpful in other fields also.

An Administrator's Procedures *

By E. M. Bluestone, M.D.

Like his fellow men, the hospital executive is humble in the face of death but, unlike his fellow men, he is confronted with this phenomenon so frequently that he is likely to reconcile himself to its repetition as if it were something that he must accept without question as inevitable.

The subject of death is often passed over quickly in hospitals in the desire to concentrate on the urgent living business at hand. There is a tendency to regard death as something of a nuisance which must be endured after failure to cure has been registered. Yet, death as well as the threat of death should have a galvanizing effect on the most phlegmatic of hospital servants. The hospital executive can, indeed, be measured by his ability to profit from each experience. Any tendency on his part to accept death as a natural phenomenon which requires no further effort or explanation is unforgiveable. The prevention of a fatal outcome is the first assignment for any hospital. This requirement is all the more significant, in that the emotion of fear is a complication of every diagnosis on the admission of a patient.

* This contribution is based on the article "On the Significance of Death in Hospital Practice" which appeared in the March 1952 issue of The Modern Hospital and is included here with permission of the journal.

Often, when death is imminent, the question arises as to how much it is good to tell the patient. There are some instances where there is something spiritual, if not material, to be gained by telling the patient how matters stand with him as the final shadows fall. However, there are more instances where something is definitely lost. The effect of the announcement on the patient himself must be paramount in our decision. To a lesser extent we must consider the effect on his family and indirectly, at times, on the community in which he moves. If we value courage in the patient we must stimulate and not depress it. If the patient is not conscious he cannot, of course, be told, but we must not be too sure of the depth of his coma. Many a dying patient has heard an intern speak the sentence in his presence, while some had the strength left to dispute him.

In each individual case we deal with an unprecedented situation. Sickness is a humiliating experience and death can become a degrading finale for sensitive human beings. Some people go through this world with an acute awareness that the life of every human being is destined to come to an end sooner or later, while others live on as if they felt themselves gifted with a charmed and endless life. Between these extremes one finds all kinds and conditions of men. The hospital executive must be a good judge of human nature to deal successfully with each instance.

Most often the time of death cannot be foretold with any degree of accuracy. Collective judgment on prognosis is desirable before any approach is made to the vexing question as to what we shall tell the patient at the end.

An important determinant may be the clinical condition which is killing the patient. If there is a virulent infection, the patient is the victim of an overwhelming toxemia which makes him oblivious to signs and symptoms. If an injury is the cause of death, severe shock enters into the picture. If it is a deformity as, for example, a congenital defect of the heart, the patient goes through life knowing that the end is always near his immediate horizon. If it is a malignant growth, he often suspects the worst, and it is his problem, in particular, which troubles us most when we ponder the question as to what he may be told.

It is preferable to tell the patient the truth than to let him discover his plight by frightening contacts, like the special death-room in the hospital, and the use of heartless designations such as "incurable," "cancer ward," and the like. The incurable patient of today may be the curable patient of tomorrow. No medical facility is in a better position to bring about this result than the modern general hospital. A diagnosis of incurability should never be made, lest we convert a possibly hopeful and curable patient into a hopeless and incurable one.

It is natural and in keeping with the best traditions of mutual aid to employ every device available in an effort to help the patient. However, since acuteness and urgency wear off before the condition is cured—provided there is to be a cure—and since illness may continue and not be as demanding in its call for help, the hospital executive must have his ears and all his other senses attuned to a call from the patient which, though subdued, may be quite ominous in its possibilities. High temperature, exsanguination or shock are not the only exciting causes of death. It can, and too often does, occur by a process of attrition, unmatched by the tenacity of the most persistent doctor. "Could another doctor do better?" is a question which every hospital executive must solve for himself, and there are times when the answer will lead him into the realm of the highest statesmanship.

Many of us working in a hospital have at one time or another considered the advisability of asking ante-mortem permission for autopsy. In most instances this would be a crude if not cruel procedure which might well destroy those very defenses which we are trying to build up in the patient and his family. It is not often that a patient is spiritually strong enough to be told, and it is rare indeed that he is strong-willed to the point where he can consider such a step. But when death strikes in spite of our best efforts, the hospital executive owes it to the dead, his family, his representatives, friends and neighbors to explain the fatal outcome in detail and, while there is yet time, make the last effort to solve a process of nature before the mystery is forever sealed up in the earth. The success of the hospital executive in winning the consent of the next of kin to post-mortem examination is, in the most profound sense of the term, a measure of his usefulness to the community.

Sympathy and Objectivity in Balance

By Eloise R. Lewis, R.N., M.S.
and Esther K. Sump, R.N., M.S.

"Should the patient know the truth" is a question that can be answered only for each individual. There cannot be one answer; no one rule should or could apply in all cases. The patient's attitude toward this question will be determined by his age, experience, endowment, philosophy, and temperament. To the patient, his illness is a very personal matter, sometimes to the apparent exclusion of all other responsibilities. The patient who has the greater spiritual resources, who has achieved inner contentment and come to terms with life and the thoughts of death may make the better adjustment to illness.

Our question primarily concerns the patient, but the attitude of the doctor, the nurse, and the family toward the situation must also be considered. In helping another person we are unable to go beyond certain limits, but these vary with his needs, fears, and doubts. We must study each individual carefully and then help him to the best of our ability. Our faith must be, as has been wonderfully said by Reinhold Niebuhr, that the Lord will give us the serenity to accept what cannot be changed, the courage to change what can be changed, and the wisdom to know one from the other. To us, this ideal includes all that one could hope to achieve in helping another human being.

Today much information concerning medical conditions, their treatment and prognosis, is made available to the public by radio, television, and the press. Through these media the patient may have acquired sufficient information to worry and to wonder, unless given all the facts by his doctor. It would be impossible to keep the truth from some patients because of their experience and knowledge. We find few people who are not suspicious of what to expect when they visit the physician or clinic. Sometimes it is more difficult to convince the patient of the truth than to dispel ideas and feelings which he has built within himself.

Patients seldom ask the direct question, "Do I have an incurable disease?" or "Am I going to die?" Often the very nature of the condition and treatment which needs the cooperation of the patient tells the story without words. It is important that the physician and the nurse have a good understanding of the patient and anticipate the reaction he may have when faced with a situation in which he must accept reality. Each patient must be considered as an individual in his own right. The emotionally mature person, for example, whose attitude is one that grows and expands with each new experience, may have more fear of uncertainty than of the truth to which he can adjust. The nurse must be able to evaluate behavior and situations, and must function intelligently and quickly in response to their variations. When nurses are in contact with patients over a period of time, they have more opportunities to observe behavior and listen to expressions of thought under varying conditions than do physicians whose contacts are intermittent and brief. It is, therefore, very important that anything the nurse does or says is based on a sound understanding of human behavior and human relationships.

Early in the experience of the nurse, she learns to be aware of the fears and anxieties which naturally beset a patient when he becomes ill, sometimes separated from his familiar surroundings and from those he loves. The first opportunity that the nurse has to "tell the truth" is when she can provide simple explanations of procedures and treatments. It is the right and privilege of every patient to know whether he is going to x-ray, to surgery, or to have a hypodermic injection; knowing these simple things frequently allays fear.

From these beginnings the nurse learns to function in the more complex situations in which she knows the doctor has told the patient that he must face an amputation, mutilating surgery, long illness, or death. She understands that a patient facing death, who has no spiritual advisor, may wish to pour out to the nurse his fears, regrets, and hopes, and she knows that she must be prepared to help him by listening with respect and sympathy. The nurse is there to help and sustain, but never to rob the patient of the use of his own resources in facing reality. She learns to think much but say little in proportion to her thoughts.

To be most helpful, the nurse must know what information the patient and his family have been given. There is a great need for more adequate communication between the doctor and nurse as to what explanation has been given and why. Only if this mutual understanding is present, will the nurse be able to emphasize what the physician deems most important and to reinforce explanations already given.

The nurse must accept and help the patient understand whatever explanation the physician has given. It is her responsibility to find the right words in answering questions and to sustain the patient's hopes and alleviate his fears to the best of her ability. The patient need not be faced with a feeling of uncertainty or hesitancy when he asks questions of the nurse that logically follow the physician's explanation. The nurse knows that tragedy seldom results when the truth has been told with adequate explanation and interpretation. Most patients, after a period of adjustment, find it possible to accept reality. Many attitudes concerning death and pain and discomfort of disease are erroneous. Some people have learned to have a reason for living rather than to be afraid of dying. The nurse must understand that there are times when the patient needs unconditional help and acceptance; at other times, freedom from all support and guidance. The effectiveness with which the nurse handles this part of her responsibility will depend to a great extent upon her understanding of the patient and his acceptance of the physician's explanation.

Because the nurse is so closely associated with the patient, her attitude and philosophy must express a concern for the fundamental needs of man. She must appreciate the worth of every human being and understand his right to a happy life; she must have a keen interest in his welfare and his adjustment; and with this spirit must go her sincere desire to help the patient.

When the patient is faced with the possibility of a physical disability or the knowledge of pending death, he must be helped to plan for this new phase of his life, whether brief or long. By working together, the nurse and the family can help the patient in gaining a new purpose and perspective of life and in adjusting to a new pattern of living.

The professional nurse will realize the importance of balancing sympathy and objectivity in meeting the needs of the patient. She must therefore cultivate her spirit and educate her heart, so that, when called upon, she is ready to give her skill, knowledge, and understanding to the patient, and to accept gratefully what he has to offer.

Ethics in Nursing Responsibility

By Sister Bernadette Armiger, R.N., M.S.

In the first moments of returning consciousness and orientation the postoperative patient frequently asks the nurse, "What did they find?" The nurse, who may know well from the diagnosis on the anesthesia sheet, usually takes refuge in a noncommittal referral to the doctor. She may add reassuring words relative to the patient's immediate postoperative condition, and utilize nursing measures to divert the still-blurred mind toward needed relaxation.

Rarely does the nurse have the responsibility of informing the patient of his condition. Her role, especially in this delicate issue, is that of assistant to the physician, supporting and sustaining his program of therapy in the hours between his visits.

However, her relationship with patients and her close observation of their reactions to illness make her keenly alive to the pros and cons of "telling the patient." Because of her strategic place at the bedside of the sick, the nurse's view and position relative to this vital subject need to be defined.

The Catholic nurse's answer to the question "Should the patient know the truth?" is formulated not only on the basis of personal opinion derived from experiential evidence but also on ethical and religious directives derived from fundamental philosophic principles.

The critically ill patient. The question has its most profound meaning in regard to the patient who is in danger of death. The principle that the Catholic nurse applies is clearly stated in the code for Catholic Hospitals:[1]

> Everyone has the right and duty to prepare for the solemn moment of death. Unless it is clear, therefore, that a dying patient is well-prepared for death, as regards both temporal and spiritual affairs, it is the physician's duty to inform, or to have some responsible person inform him, of his critical condition.

The rational patient in a normal state of mental health has a moral right to be told that his condition is serious, because he cannot prepare spiritually and materially for his exodus from life unless he knows. This does not mean knowing the precise nature of the illness leading to death. In fact, there is definitely no moral obligation to tell the exact diagnosis to the word-conscious patient when such information is not needed to assist in preparing well for death. The decision to inform the incurable patient of the precise nature of his illness rests with the physician who will be guided by his knowledge of the individual patient and by the pertinence of information to the cure, alleviation, or prevention of disease.

The code places the responsibility for apprising the patient of his serious state on the physician, primarily, though he may delegate this duty to a member of the family, a close friend or business associate, the hospital chaplain, a nursing sister, or a nurse, if he believes that one of these can impart the news with less emotional reaction. Because of the implicit contract between the doctor and the patient, the attending physician is usually the one best qualified to approach the patient on this subject most effectively and acceptably.

The well-known moralist, Rev. Francis J. Connell, C.SS.R.,[2] affirms that the doctor has the responsibility to inform the family of the condition of a sick member:

> The Catholic doctor attending a Catholic patient is bound to inform the members of the family, so that the spiritual needs of the sick person may be provided for, and if the admonition is unheeded, the doctor has the obligation to summon the priest himself. In the case of non-Catholics, too, the doctor is bound in charity to see that the dying person prepares his soul for the supreme moment on which his lot will depend for all eternity.

Thus, it is an obligation in charity and justice to warn the patient in danger of death. A distinction must be made between the meaning of "danger of death" in medical parlance and in Church law. Medically, the phrase implies that death is imminent, while in Church law it comprises any state in which there is reasonable expectation that death may ensue from a patient's condition even though death is not expected in a matter of hours.

The nurse must be aware that the Catholic patient in danger of death, from whatever cause, is bound by precept to receive Holy Viaticum and Extreme Unction if possible while in full possession of his rational faculties. The sacraments must never be deferred until the patient has lapsed into unconsciousness.

This poses the problem of nurse's responsibility if the doctor refuses to tell the patient that death is imminent and involves the family in the conspiracy of silence. Should the nurse adhere to the doctor's policy if her religious convictions stress that one is bound in conscience to tell the patient when death is an immediate possibility?

Is this question a matter of choice or of obligation? If the nurse cannot influence the doctor or get his permission that she suggests to relatives to tell, then she has the right and duty to consult proper authority within the hospital administration or medical staff organization. Under their guidance she may present the problem to the patient's clergyman so that he may assume responsibility.

As a rule, the nurse's role consists in informing the patient in danger of death that the doctor considers it advisable for him to receive the Last Sacraments or, in the case of a non-Catholic, the consolations of his clergyman. If the physician has paved the way by speaking in a straightforward manner of the seriousness of the patient's condition, the nurse, by her calm matter-of-fact attitude, can further help the patient in accepting religious succor. This is her opportunity to bring into full play what the nursing profession so glibly calls "nursing the whole patient." As the things of Time recede and Eternity approaches, spiritual values assume their true proportion. The patient should be encouraged to conform his will to the Divine Will in his sufferings, and make of his last hours a harvest time for heaven. It is comforting to the dying patient to have a nurse who is able to speak simply and familiarily of serious subjects, one who without words, too, conveys spiritual comfort. Ordinarily, nursing care is directed toward helping the patient to recover and face life again. Nurses meet a greater challenge when helping a human being to face death, serenely and confidently.

The curable patient. The Catholic nurse has also specific directives to guide her in her answer to the question, "Should the curable patient know the truth?" Rev. Gerald Kelly, S.J., states that the patient should be given whatever information is needed to enable him to cooperate intelligently with the physician.[3] The doctor, in this case, too, determines on the basis of his knowledge of the patient's intelligence, emotional stability, and reaction to past crises whether or not the patient should know the truth, and to what extent he should be informed.

Knowledge basic to consent. It is a principle of the natural law that everyone is constituted the administrator of his own life and health. When a patient places himself under the care of a physician, he implicitly consents to the ordinary diagnostic and therapeutic measures employed. During preoperative preparation the patient may have many questions about the various tests to which he is subjected. Such a request for knowledge is reasonable, but it is not the nurse's prerogative to interpret the meaning or usefulness of the tests in reference to diagnoses. She may give only such information as will facilitate the patient's understanding of his part in the procedures. By simple explanations she may familiarize him with necessary details of the new experience so that he will have some awareness of what will take place, who will be there, and what he should do. Beyond this it is the nurse's duty to report the patient's queries to the physician who may judge whether to give the information sought or permit the nurse to give an accurate answer.

If the means taken for cure involves serious hazard to life, for example, heart surgery, the patient should know the risk involved because he is not required to accept extraordinary means to preserve his life. Confronted with an operation resulting in serious changes in form and function, the patient has the right to know the nature and probable outcome of surgery, before he consents to the procedure. Consent is a free, rational act which supposes knowledge of that to which consent is given. Acquiescence cannot be voluntary unless the patient has been apprised of the serious consequences. The information given need not be precise, but it should be substantially correct.[4]

The nurse is frequently called upon to listen while a patient talks out his fears and forebodings regarding pending surgery. Willingness to listen is important, while attempts to "quiet" the patient on the assumption that he will get more upset if he talks about his condition seldom abate anxiety. In talking to the patient, the nurse and other members of the health team should avoid over-reassurance and over-explanation.

The postoperative patient. Not infrequently a surgeon determines that the patient, because of emotional lability, should not know his postoperative diagnosis. In this case the patient's best interests may be served by concealing or minimizing the seriousness of a condition that does not have dangerous consequences. The patient will be told only what may be necessary to encourage him to cooperate in his care. The nurse will hide the truth, but she is never permitted to lie to the patient when she is faced with a direct question concerning diagnosis. Lying is intrinsically evil because it is wrong to use the faculty of speech in such a manner as to frustrate its natural end, the communication of ideas.

What is the nurse to do when the gynecological patient asks after surgery, "Will I be able to become pregnant again?" The nurse who knows that the uterus was removed, but who was not present at the operation, may truthfully say, "I was not in the operating room. Your doctor will tell you about it when he visits you." Moralists allege that the nurse does not offend against veracity when, without saying something that is false, she answers in a way that does not give information which should be concealed. A nurse may not always respond astutely when such occasions arise, but if she habitually reconstructs the situations which challenge her to reconcile professional secrecy and truth, she will develop ability to respond prudently and tactfully, yet withal to the patient's satisfaction.

This mode of speaking can only be used lawfully when (1) it gives some hint by words or circumstances of the true meaning; (2) there is grave reason for concealment; and (3) the intention of the speaker is honest—not to deceive but to preserve information which he or she is bound to keep concealed.[5] Under these conditions the nurse can withhold information provided there is no violation of the justice due to the patient.

Effect on the patient. The deleterious effects of not telling the truth are evidenced by the patient's loss of faith in those who by reason of their profession should be his strongest allies in illness.

The patient is usually alert to the slightest hesitation in a doctor's answer to a direct or indirect question about diagnosis. Even the semblance of a suspicion that the physician is not telling the truth engenders an unwholesome state of mind in which doubt and fear supplant faith and trust. The patient in his anxiety-ridden state may confide to the nurse fears that are more devastating than the true condition. A patient who does not expose his doubts and worries verbally often gives the clue to his mental disquiet by the clinical manifestations of anxiety which defy nursing ministrations and hinder medical therapy.

The therapeutic value of knowledge of the truth about his condition varies from one patient to the other. With certain unstable individuals, the potential mental and emotional reactions to such information preclude any positive benefit. On the other hand, a calm, common-sense, solidly religious patient may be told with profit.

The decision to tell involves the contingent questions of when, what, and how. The propitious moment for telling the surgical patient may be prior to the operation if there is little possibility of doubt as to the extent of surgery; for other patients it may be after the pathologic report has been prepared. In most cases the doctor should build up to the statement and give the patient time to think over the matter and to discuss his ideas in subsequent interviews. The nurse should certainly be permitted to share the onus of dealing with the patient's dawning realization of all that is entailed in such knowledge. Efficient teamwork is possible only if there is a mutual sharing of information between doctor and nurse.

What to tell. The simplest guide for determining what to tell is the specific question the patient is asking; the answer is modified by the doctor's discretion. Often, the extent of information given depends upon what the patient already knows through social contacts and public education. The nurse has a role here, too. She is frequently asked questions which the patient, because he is embarrassed or fears to appear ignorant, avoids submitting to the doctor. Many misconceptions can be eradicated by the nurse who is able to supply sound facts in an unhurried, understanding manner.

How to tell. The most important aspect of informing the patient of the truth is how to tell. The feeling of inadequacy or an excessive identification with the patient will hamper the telling, while simple clear statements generate confidence and calm. In telling the patient, the doctor is acting with authority and full recognition of his spiritual responsibility to the patient who has entrusted him with his life. Knowing human error, there can never be finality or time-table prognostication in the truth told. A warm, personal manner conveys the feeling of professional acceptance and support as well as the assurance that positive contributions to the patient's physical well-being will be made to alleviate mental and physical distress. Likewise, the knowledge that the family, the nurse, and other members of the health team will be given careful and detailed directions insures coordinated action in the therapeutic program.

Sparing the patient knowledge of the truth savors of misguided sentimentality and false humanitarianism.

REFERENCES

1. Ethical and Religious Directives for Catholic Hospitals. St. Louis, The Catholic Hospital Association, 1949, p. 3.
2. Connell, F. J.: Morals in Politics and Professions. Westminster, Md., The Newman Bookshop, 1946, pp. 122 f.
3. Kelly, G.: Should the Cancer Patient Be Told? Medico-Moral Problems, Part II. St. Louis, The Catholic Hospital Association, 1950, pp. 8 f.
4. Kelly, G.: Consent of the patient. Hospital Progress *32*:305, 1951.
5. McAllister, J. B.: Ethics. Philadelphia, Saunders, 1947, p. 299.

ADDITIONAL BIBLIOGRAPHY

Bonner, A.: The Catholic Doctor. London, Burns, Oates and Washbourne Ltd., 1939.

Coppens, C.: Moral Principles and Medical Practice. New York, Benziger Brothers, 1897.

FITTS, W. T., AND RAVDIN, I. S.: What Philadelphia physicians tell patients with cancer. J.A.M.A. *153*:901, 1953.

GUENTHER, V., AND OTHERS: Letter to the medical staff of Mercy Hospital. The Linacre Quarterly *20*:48, 1953.

GREGG, D. E.: Anxiety. A factor in nursing care. Am. J. Nursing *52*:1363, 1952.

HEALY, E. F.: Moral Guidance. Chicago, Loyola University Press, 1942.

HIGGINS, T. J.: Man as Man. Milwaukee, The Bruce Publishing Company, 1949.

KENNY, J. P.: Principles of Medical Ethics. Westminster, Md., Newman Press, 1952.

MCFADDEN, C. J.: Medical Ethics, 2nd ed. Philadelphia. F. A. Davis Company, 1949.

POPE PIUS XII: Moral limits of medical research and treatment. English translation of allocution "Ce Premier Congres." The Catholic Mind *51*:305, 1953.

ROTONDI, A. J.: Relations between the chaplain and the hospital staff. The Linacre Quarterly *20*:71, 1953.

ROTUNDI, A. J.: Should doctors tell? America *90*:219, November 28, 1953.

ROTUNDI, A. J.: Should the incurables be told "bitter" truth? The Pilot, Boston, April 10, 1954.

SHOULD THE PATIENT KNOW THE TRUTH?

The Priest's Response

By John A. Goodwine, S.T.L., J.C.D.

There are two aspects of this question that I shall treat separately. The first is the more general and I have phrased it: "Should the patient be informed of the approach of death?" The other is more particular and, I suspect, more provocative of discussion: "Should the patient know the precise nature of his disease? Should he be told, for example, he has cancer?"

On the first question, I think the position of Catholic moralists may be summarized in the words of the Ethical and Religious Code for Catholic Hospitals, that every person has the right and the duty to prepare for the solemn moment of death.*

According to Catholic belief, at the moment of death the soul leaves the body and appears before its Creator to receive from Him the sentence of eternal reward or eternal punishment. If the soul, when it leaves this world, is in a state of friendship with God, that is, if it is in sanctifying grace, it will be saved; but if it is in mortal sin and consequently in a state of hostility toward God, it will be lost. It is, therefore, tremendously important that a patient about to pass into eternity be given the opportunity of preparing himself for that momentous event.

For a Catholic patient this preparation will consist

* Quoted more fully in Sister Bernadette's discussion.

principally in receiving the Last Sacraments of his Church. These sacraments have the power of removing guilt of sin and of restoring the soul to the friendship of God, provided the patient is truly repentant. They strengthen the soul for the ordeal of meeting its Maker and Judge in the next world. To be fully effective, the sacraments must be received while the patient is conscious and aware that he is receiving them. Consequently, the patient who is approaching death should be advised of his critical situation.

The physician has an obligation, based on the brotherhood of man, to prevent harm from befalling his patient insofar as he can do so without himself suffering serious hardship. For a doctor to "protect" a patient so effectively that the patient slips out of this life without realizing it may, in reality, be a cruel deception; for it may expose the patient to the danger of losing his immortal soul.

The physician, however, will have performed his duty if he has informed the family of the patient's condition, or if he has advised them to call the priest. It may often be better that the family tell the patient, which is less apt to be frightening, than if the information were to come from the physician. The patient is more likely to receive it as the expression of anxious solicitude than as a sentence of death.

The doctor himself will have to inform the patient, if there is no one able or willing to send for the priest, or if the patient will not believe anyone but his doctor regarding the seriousness of his condition. If the physician knows that the patient has already prepared himself for death as regards both temporal and spiritual affairs, he need not issue any warning at all.

It will be the physician's duty to remain silent if a

warning will do the patient more harm than good. For instance, a doctor may have good reason to fear, in a particular case, that information about the patient's condition will bring on a fit of despair which might lead to something worse. However, I feel that the physician ought not to give in too readily to the fear that knowledge of approaching death will unduly excite or depress the patient. I have never met a dying Catholic who became overly excited when he saw me enter his room to administer the Last Sacraments. The coming of the priest may excite the relatives, but it brings solace and consolation to the dying patient. Doctors themselves have often expressed their surprise that the sick so eagerly welcome the suggestion that they should receive the sacraments. Moreover, the reception of the Sacraments almost always brings calmness, serenity, and peace which the doctor will feel gratified to have procured for his patient.

Turning to the second phase of our problem, "Should the cancer patient know the truth?" I should, at the start, point out that Catholic moralists have no clear-cut answer applicable to all cases. Nor do I think that such an answer is possible. I cannot agree with those who would maintain that a doctor should in every case explain to the patient the exact nature of his disease, so that failure to do this would be considered morally wrong. Nor would I agree that the doctor should always withhold such information. I feel that the answer will depend on circumstances, psychological, legal, moral, medical, financial, and perhaps others. Circumstances differ according to individuals. It is quite possible that in one case the physician has a duty to inform his patient, while in the next case his duty is to maintain a discreet silence. The criterion ought to be the patient's welfare, but I admit that it is not always easy to see in what direction the patient's welfare lies.

Obviously, it would be morally wrong for the physician to cause harm or damage to his patient. In some cases, failure to advise the patient of the full truth will prove seriously harmful. An extreme example of this would be the physician who, by holding out false hopes of recovery, induces the patient to undergo expensive treatments which the physician recognizes to be useless. In other cases a full explanation of the nature of the patient's disease may cause more harm than good. Then the physician would be wise to withhold all or at least part of the truth.

The moralist, however, is concerned chiefly with the possibility of spiritual harm arising from the physician's failure to inform his patient adequately regarding his condition. We have discussed the patient's right to know the seriousness of his condition so that he may prepare for death, and the physician's duty to provide him with that information. Applying that to the present problem, I should say that the patient for whom there is no hope of recovery should know the truth, *if* ignorance could result in serious spiritual harm. A patient with an incurable cancer, for example, would certainly suffer spiritual harm if his physician should feed him with false hopes of recovery to such an extent that he fails to prepare his soul to meet his Judge. If the patient also neglects to take care of his temporal affairs, by making a will, for instance, the physician's neglect to inform him of the true state of affairs could be morally culpable on this score also.

Accordingly, a Catholic patient for whom there is no hope of recovery must be advised of his critical condition in plenty of time to allow for the fruitful reception of the

Last Sacraments. Others, who are not Catholics, must be allowed to make whatever preparation their consciences demand. The physician is allowed, indeed he must use his good judgment as to when, how, and under what circumstances he will advise the family or the patient of the situation. I think the doctor is not obliged to inform the patient of the exact nature of his disease. Sometimes no real benefit can be derived from telling a patient that he has cancer; often actual harm may result. In such cases, the physician's duty may be to refrain from giving the information.

As for the so-called curable cases, e.g., cancer patients for whom there is at least some hope of recovery, the moralist would go along with those who say the patient should be given whatever information is necessary for him to cooperate intelligently with the physician. The application of this principle will vary in individual cases because of psychologic factors. One patient may cooperate splendidly if told he has cancer. Another patient may have such a horror of the disease as to make him look upon recovery as a mere delusion. Once again, the physician will have to use his judgment and evaluate his patient carefully before giving him information.

The Rabbi's Response

By Louis I. Newman, Ph.D., D.D.

The views of Jewish religio-ethical writers and physicians on the question, "Shall the patient be told the truth?" may be said to reflect the varying opinions among persons of other liberal faiths. Throughout the centuries, the subject has been discussed both directly and indirectly from a number of viewpoints, and the literature of Judaism furnishes data regarding these manifold opinions.

By and large it may be affirmed that most Jewish teachers and physicians have held the opinion that utmost consideration must be shown for the patient; that his well-being should be the primary factor in determining the information, if any, to be given him regarding his illness.

Reverence for the physician has been characteristic of the Jewish people throughout the centuries. During the Middle Ages Jewish physicians were highly respected and sought out, even by the adversaries of Judaism and Jewry, and they served to introduce into the Western world much of the scientific knowledge current among Arab physicians and scientists. It is not surprising therefore that the patient in the Jewish community should lean upon the ministration of the physician or surgeon. He takes it for granted that the doctor is seeking to do all in his power to cure him or to prolong his life. Moreover, the patient wishes to believe that his doctor will not needlessly cause him distress of spirit or fatal anxiety.

Thus in the Midrash,[1] the ancient homiletic exegesis of the Torah (the Holy Law of Jewish tradition), we find the words:

> Even when the physician sees that death is approaching, he still says to the patient, "Eat this and abstain from that; drink this, and not that;" but he does not say, "Your end is near," and he rebukes the prophet Isaiah in the name of King Hezekiah for telling him bluntly, "Set thy house in order for thou shalt die and not live." (II Kings 20:1).

An aphorism of Isaac Solomon Israeli,[2] a physician of the 9th and 10th century of Mauretania and Cyrenaica, declared:

> Try to ease the mind of the patient; encourage him to look forward to being cured, even if thou art not thyself convinced of it, for this will surely strengthen his nature.

Consideration for the sick person is the rule in Jewish religious life. Thus in the *Kitzur Shulhan Arukh*[3] (the standard Jewish law code for traditionalist Jews, compiled about 1564-65) it is provided:

> If an experienced physician, although he be a non-Jew, or another one who understands, says that although the sick person is in no immediate danger, the sickness may nevertheless assume a dangerous form unless a certain remedy is applied therefore, even if the invalid says that if a certain remedy will not be applied, he will surely die, but if applied there is a chance that he might live, the Sabbath should also be disregarded. (Kitzur Shulhan Arukh, xcii, 3).

A religious precept can be transgressed for the sake of the patient's welfare. It is customary "to bless the sick person in the synagogue, and if he be dangerously ill, he is blessed even on the Sabbath, and a Festival. At the time the name of the sick person is changed." (Kitzur Shulhan Arukh, cxci, 2).

In the regulations concerning visiting of the sick, the rules are so developed that one should not "spoil (the patient's) chance of recovery by casting upon him the designation of an invalid." (*Ibid.*, cxciii, 1).

> He who visits the sick frequently is praiseworthy providing he should not become troublesome to the invalid. (*Ibid.*, 3).
>
> All who visit the sick person should speak to him with judgment and tact; they should speak in such a manner so as neither to revive him (with false hopes) nor to depress him (by words of despair), but they should tell him to concern himself with his affairs, indicating that if he had granted a loan to others, or had deposited anything with others or others with him (he should mention the fact). The sick person should not fear on this account that he will die. (*Ibid.*, 5).
>
> A sick person who desires to make a transfer of his property by symbolical ceremony of acquiring possession in order to confirm his will may do so even on the Sabbath; if he desires to send for his relatives, he may hire a non-Jew on the Sabbath and send him. (*Ibid.*, 8).
>
> If a member of the family of the invalid has died he should not be informed thereof lest it may worry him, and even if he became aware thereof he should not be told to rend his garment (the ceremony of Ker'iah), lest it increase his distress. One should neither weep nor mourn in the presence of the sick person, whether the dead be a member of the sick person's family or a stranger, lest he fear that he also will die. All who comfort mourners in the presence of the sick person should be compelled to remain silent. (*Ibid.*, 9).

Through the medium of the Viddui, the confession, it

is possible to bring home to the patient gently and with kindliness the danger of his condition.

> If the visitors perceive that he, the invalid, is dying, they should tactfully turn the conversation so that they are led to tell him to confess and they should add, "Do not fear that evil will ensue, for many who have confessed became well and did not die, and there were many who did not confess and died. On the contrary, as a reward for having confessed, thy life may be prolonged. Moreover all who confess have a share in the World-to-Come." If he be unable to confess verbally, he should make a mental confession, and if he be able to speak but little, he should be told to say, "May my death atone for all my sins." The sick person should also be reminded to ask the pardon of all against whom he had sinned, whether in material matters or by words. These words should not be spoken in the presence of ignorant women and children, for it may cause them to cry and make the sick person broken-hearted. (*Ibid.*, 13). If he desires to prolong the confession in a similar manner to the confession on the Day of Atonement, he is permitted to do so. (*Ibid.*, 14).

A description has been published[4] of the ritual practiced in Furth, Germany, in the 18th century, according to the Refuat Neshamah (Medicine for the Soul). It follows, in general, the guidance furnished by the Shulhan Arukh, as outlined above. The visitor to the sick always speaks encouragingly to the patient to dispel his fear. He then suggests to the patient that, although he is in no danger, he ought be mindful of the injunctions of the Rabbis to show evidence of repentance and good deeds, in order to stand before the divine judgment; he also ought to place his business affairs in order and make a will. Usually a friend approached him in these delicate matters. The patient was enjoined to make peace with any person with whom he may have had a dispute; he was asked to make a donation to charity and was advised to instruct his heirs to make certain charitable bequests, even though he might not be in danger of dying.

Thus, it may be affirmed that in Jewish tradition there was an earnest desire to spare the feeling of the sick person to the utmost and to bear in mind his welfare above all else. As far as possible the information of the fatal nature of the illness was not given unless or until it was necessary to do so. The religious tradition of Jewry ordained, that as much compassion as possible should be shown to the afflicted person, in accordance with the realities of the entire situation. A Talmudic tractate throws light on the question whether it is permissible, from the religious point of view, to modify the truth in speaking to a patient about his condition. One teacher takes the stand that, for the sake of peace, it is quite proper to withhold the truth in its entirety. Another teacher goes even further, saying that, for the sake of peace, it is our duty not to reveal the whole truth. Both of these statements are fortified by a so-called Baraita (a tradition of teachings by certain Sages known as the Tannaim not included in the Mishnah, but assembled in a separate collection) which declares that God Himself, not to cause ill-will to arise between Abraham and Sarah, deliberately did not reproduce with accuracy one of the utterances of Sarah. According to Jewish scholars these precedents justify the physician or a member of the family in softening the truth when speaking to the patient regarding the possible or probable consequences of his malady.

To this very day, even though the rituals and prayers of the traditional guidebooks are not well known to modern-minded Jews, they have nevertheless a tradition and an intuition regarding these matters, based upon the tender and merciful approach of classic Judaism.

Without doubt, the person possessed of the fortitude which a philosophy of life or a religious faith conveys to him is prepared for any and every emergency. "The readiness is all," says Hamlet. A vigorous personality, whether of secular or pious inclinations, may be geared to the shock of being notified that he is the victim of an ailment which will soon terminate his life. Such a person, with reasonable serenity of spirit, sets his house in order; makes his peace with society and girds himself for the inevitable. The more sensitive person may not be able to demonstrate a similar courage; he may hug to himself the illusion that he will grow well; that perhaps a miracle of healing will occur, even though the Shulhan Arukh (cxii, 3) forbids a man who is in danger to rely upon a miracle. Such a person may give an indication of his awareness of what is ahead, but only obliquely and indirectly. The doctor, therefore, does well to suit his approach to the temperament that the individual patient has. If there is nothing to be gained by informing the patient of the actual circumstances, the doctor wisely may forbear. But if it is necessary to announce, however delicately, the ominous tidings, this should be done in consultation with the family. No doctor, worthy of his great calling, is brutally frank without regard for the sensibilities of the patient and his kinsfolk. Moreover, the wise doctor employs discretion as to the timing and setting of the occasion when he tells the patient. The doctor may find it impossible to act in conformity with a fixed principle or procedure; he must be thoroughly pragmatic, erring on the side of mercy.

The easiest patient to deal with in his ultimate crisis

is, oftentimes, not so much the deeply pious as the sincerely religious person who believes that "the Eternal God is a dwelling-place;" who realizes, as a Talmudic passage declares, that "for all creatures death has been prepared from the beginning" (*Tanh.B.*, Wa-ethanan, 6a). He shares the attitude of Rabbi Ben Karshook (immortalized in a poem by Robert Browning) who told his disciples they should repent one day before their death. When they inquired how they might know the day of their death, he answered they should repent every day. The literature of the Hasidic Rabbis in the 18th and 19th centuries contains many examples of the calm of the saintly in the presence of imminent death.

To persons of sublime bravery and faith, the physician will convey, with a minimum of difficulty, the message of the approaching Angel of Death. Ordinary men and women may not possess a similar faculty for resignation to the Will of the Universe, yet it is commended to all. It behooves everyone who can manifest the mood of reconciliation to heed the words of Sirach (41:1-4) who declares:

> Be not afraid of the death that is decreed for thee; remember that the generations, former and later, are in the same case with thee. This is the lot of all flesh by the Lord's appointment, and why shouldst thou set thyself against the will of the Most High?

REFERENCES

1. FRIEDENWALD, H.: The Jews and Medicine, Essays. Baltimore, Johns Hopkins Press, 1947. Vol. I. p. 19.
2. Ibid. p. 25.
3. Kitzur Shulhan Arukh. A Compilation of Jewish Laws and Customs, by Rabbi Solomon Ganzfried, translated by Hyman E. Goldin. New York, Hebrew Publishing Company, 1927.
4. MARCUS, J. R.: Communal Sick-Care in the German Ghetto. Chapter on The Spiritual Care. Cincinnati, Hebrew Union College Press, 1944.
5. Babylonian Talmud. Yebamot 65b.

The Minister's Response

By J. V. Langmead Casserley, D.Litt.

Whether it is true or not, the impression is certainly widespread in the public mind that medical men often mislead their patients into supposing that the condition of their health is less serious than it really is. In particular, it is commonly said, physicians are disinclined to give any clear warning to sick people that their life's end is approaching. It is, of course, supposed that the intention of the physician in misleading patients in this way is to spare them mental pain and distress, and, further, that most physicians approve of such a practice on ethical grounds. Indeed, many non-medical people themselves approve of what they imagine to be standard medical practice.

I think it would be idle to pretend that this general impression has no basis in fact whatsoever. It is probable that most of us have known cases in which the truth was withheld from friends and relatives of our own in precisely this way. Sometimes we ourselves have cooperated with the doctor in this merciful withholding of what most of us feel would be gloomy information.

My own experience during the years that I acted as a hospital chaplain has given me the impression that this strategy does not always succeed. Very often the dying patient does somehow feel within himself that the end is near and he plays a part in the grizzly comedy of pretending that things are better with him than they are. His friends around his bedside assure him that he will be up and about again very shortly, and he pretends that for his part he is feeling better already. So they all conspire together to avoid bringing up, in so many words, the dark subject of their impending separation.

It is not only death which the doctor avoids mentioning. The very name of certain diseases has such a depressing emotional effect on many people that the physician or surgeon will avoid using such dreaded words when diagnosing their maladies. This practice has several unintended consequences. It is so well known that cancer patients are not usually told that they are suffering from cancer, that quite a number of people who have no cancer are inwardly convinced that they do have it and that they are being deceived in the same way as they have known other people to be deceived in the past.

I have met, in surgical wards, people not suffering from cancer who were haunted by the fear that they were suffering from cancer, and who would not and could not accept any assurance to the contrary. Cancer is presumably the most striking example but not the only one. The emotional reactions to all the ills crudely lumped together under the heading of "heart disease" are not dissimilar.

Thus the practice of restraint in the imparting of information, however merciful the motive, may have the unfortunate result of breaking the general faith of the patient in what the doctor says. However reassuringly he may speak, there often lingers in the mind of the sick man the suspicion that perhaps the doctor is doing no more than trying to be kind and sparing him the knowledge of the grim truth.

It must be confessed that this kind of restraint in communicating the truth does not fit the Christian tradition too well. According to that tradition, man has the right to the truth, and his right to the truth is part of his dignity as a human being. "Things are what they are," said the great eighteenth-century Bishop Butler, "and they will be what they will be. Why then should we ask to be deceived?" From the Christian point of view, men ought not to be afraid of death, and they ought to find within themselves the spiritual resources which would enable them to withstand and bear with dignity the news that death is approaching. But in our world things are not always as they ought to be. I believe that many people, if they were consulted beforehand, would ask to be deceived, and that many do lack the spiritual resources to face the fact of impending death with confidence and faith and hope. This means that the doctor, when making up his mind as to whether or not he should tell the whole truth in any particular case, has to try to make a judgment about the psychological and spiritual condition of the patient with whom he has to do. Probably some people ought to be told and can be told without serious consequences. Others, however, could not bear the news, and it is perhaps more merciful to spare them.

I remember a Swiss physician practicing in Geneva telling me that he had a very simple rule which guided his conduct in this matter. "I always tell Catholics," he said, "but I never tell Protestants." He was himself a Protestant, so that there is no question of religious bias here. He was aware of the fact that among Catholic Christians there are things to be done at the time of death which all Catholics believe to be important. The Protestant tradition, on the other hand, lacks any kind of insistence on surrounding the death-bed with particular rites and ceremonies which give dignity to death and express its meaning. It is certainly true that when something positive has to be done at the time of death there is less danger of morbid broodings and emotional consequences that needlessly distress all concerned.

We can ask, therefore, of the medical man that in certain specific cases he should be frank and open with his patient; but we cannot reasonably expect that he should take upon himself the responsibility of positively assuring any man that he is about to die. My experience is that most physicians will admit that they have at times been mistaken. A physician may often be assured in his own mind that death in some particular case may be overwhelmingly probable, but he can rarely, perhaps never, be absolutely certain. He cannot say of a patient or to a patient that he is "going to die very shortly." He can say that his medical skill and knowledge are exhausted, and that he cannot suggest any further measures to restore the patient to health; that, therefore, the patient, who has lived his life in the knowledge that he will die some day, must face the probability that that day is now near at hand, and make himself ready to depart in a manner that befits the teaching and tradition of his religious faith. Any man of religious conviction and spiritual maturity may rightfully expect such advice from his physician; but more than that we cannot demand.

I do not think it possible to lay down any definite ethical law about a question so delicate as this. The doctor, after all, is a kind of pastor, and a wise pastor treats the human beings under his care as he finds them. He will feel almost certain that some human beings must be spared the truth that death is near. We may remember the words of Jesus, "I have yet many things to tell you, but you cannot bear them now." But quite certainly some other human beings must be told, and to tell them is a tribute to the dignity and maturity as human beings to which, inspired by their religious faith, they have attained.

Conflict of Considerations

By Bruno Furst, LL.D.

The law does not say that the doctor must tell his patient everything about imminent death and it does not forbid him to do so. The doctor must follow his conscience. Though we all know that we have to die sooner or later, the question carries a tremendous weight. In order to realize why this is so we have only to think of capital punishment. It cannot be death which makes it so frightening since the electric chair is the easiest way to die; it is the knowledge of an exact date, of the unalterable fact that it is now only one week, three days, one day until the final hour. Von Liszt, a famous Professor of Law at Berlin University, once remarked that he would certainly prefer a quick death to a lifetime behind iron bars but would tell the judge to ask him again a few minutes before the hour of death.

Obviously, the physician must be absolutely sure of his diagnosis before the question can even arise whether or not he should speak to his patient about certain death. But let's assume he is absolutely sure. Should he then tell his patient? The decision depends on the circumstances of the individual case. The real difficulty arises when spiritual considerations conflict with materialistic ones.

The physician must know whether the patient is a religious man. It does not matter which religion he belongs to. What matters is his belief in Providence and in the "other world." The man who is deeply convinced that nothing happens without the will of God will not be afraid to die. The man who deeply believes that there is a better world after death will have no fear to leave his earthly surroundings.

Next to religion, the patient's entire outlook on life must be considered. If he thinks that he lived a full life, that he has reached the goal he set for himself, he may not see any reason for staying longer on this earth. This holds true especially for somebody who was successful in his profession, business, or occupation, but was forced to retire by old age or illness. He may see little sense in living on without the responsibilities, duties, and satisfactions of his former work. The situation may be similar when a husband or wife dies. The more each meant to the other, the greater the emptiness that threatens the survivor. The wish to follow the deceased may be stronger than anything else.

A similar effect may be caused by severe pain. Illness may reach a point when even the strongest pain-killers will not help. If a patient suffers constantly and without any hope for the future, he may sincerely wish to die.

In all these cases where the patient has no fear of death, faces death as inevitable, or welcomes death there is no reason for the physician to conceal the truth; he may tell his patient that there is no hope left.

The doctor, however, in his decision, cannot ignore certain materialistic considerations. Suppose, for instance, he knows that the patient did not write a will, though the circumstances in the family are such that the will is mandatory. A patient may be aware of the necessity but may think that there is no hurry. The family doctor who has the patient's full confidence should tell him that his days are numbered and that he had better see his lawyer to have his estate distributed the way he wishes and not the way it would go without a will.

Similarly, a patient may think of starting a new enterprise which requires a large part of his financial resources and would rest primarily on his personal abilities or connections. The doctor who hears about these plans should ask himself: "Would the patient go ahead if he knew that he could not live longer than six months or a year?" If the answer is definitely "No," the physician should take this into consideration in his decision.

Or, again, a patient who lives in a big city intends to move to the country; he would be far away from specialists and hospitals but, to the doctor's knowledge, he may urgently need them in the very near future. The answer to the question, "Would the patient make such a move if he knew the truth about his health?" will direct his physician.

We may also think of the patient who does not have a family to care for him in his old age. Knowing that he must rely on his savings, he may live very economically to make his bank account last for ten or twenty years to come. If he knew that he had only one or two years to live he would perhaps prefer to do things he had always liked to do but could not afford because the thought of his old age prevented him from spending the money. Couldn't the doctor tell him the truth and by doing so make the remaining months or years more enjoyable?

But perhaps this particular patient is afraid of dying and the thought that his death is imminent would make it impossible for him to enjoy anything, even life itself. Should the physician still tell him the truth? Such, typically, are the conflicting circumstances which make a physician's decision difficult. Sometimes it may be possible to find a middle-of-the-road device, to hint to the patient that he "may" not have much longer to live. But ordinarily the easy way out is blocked by forceful considerations, and the doctor must rely on his conscience whether or not to tell his patient the truth.

If There Were a Law

By Richard M. Honig, Dr.jur.

The problem discussed in this book shall be approached here from the juridical point of view. Since there does not exist any statutory or customary law which offers a solution to it, we have to turn to the more fundamental question of how the legislator would act if he would think it necessary to establish a rule applicable to this problem. He would deduce such a rule from principles recognized for cases analogous or at least similar to our problem.

There are two groups of professionals whose rights and duties place them just between official and private persons, the lawyers and the physicians. Both act when asked to take care of the needs or worries of their clients. The confidence which their clients show in them obliges the physician as well as the lawyer to observe secrecy in regard to the facts they learn from their clients. Special circumstances, however, may oblige them to inform another person of these facts. The physician is bound, for instance, to notify the Board of Health of certain contagious diseases. Besides, he may legally be obliged to give warning to the betrothed concerning a venereal disease of his patient. In the former case it is the welfare of the public, in the latter case the health of another individual which, from the legal point of view, is of predominant importance when compared with the patient's interest in the secrecy of his disease.

In contrast to these cases, we are concerned with the question whether the patient *himself* "should know the truth." In legal terms, this phrase implies whether, or under which circumstances, the physician is obliged to inform the patient of the nature of his illness. In order to answer this question not according to our individual and vacillating sentiments but led by principles of juridical thought, we will analyze more closely the relation between the physician and his patient. Typical cases will guide us.

As long as the condition of the patient is such that the physician can cure him, the physician is obliged to do all that is necessary to improve and restore his patient's health. If, however, the physician decides on surgery as the best method of treatment, he is not authorized to proceed unless he has first secured his patient's consent. By operating he cannot avoid injuring the patient's body and will often cause permanent physical changes. If the patient is a minor, or mentally infirm, or insane, the physician's right to operate on the patient depends upon the consent of his legal representative.

From the legal point of view, an abortion induced by the physician is an operation, too. He is not entitled to act against the will of the pregnant woman.

When a patient's life is endangered by a disease that is progressive unless brought under control, to tell the patient the truth might deprive him of the spiritual energy necessary for recovery. Should such a reaction be an established medical experience, the physician is obliged *not* to inform the patient of the nature of the disease.

We turn now to the case in which the patient cannot

be saved. Two situations are to be distinguished. In the first, the patient is on the point of death, and the physician might feel induced or might be asked to relieve the agony by applying a fatal drug (euthanasia). Such action by the physician is considered legally illicit since it infringes man's "inalienable right of life."

Supposing, however, the patient, though incurably sick, may still have a chance to live for quite a while. In this event a juridical answer to the question, "Should the patient know the truth?" has not yet been established. One is prone, therefore, to solve this problem on ethical principles. Since these differ no less from one another than the philosophies of life from which they are derived, the moral standpoints of physicians differ widely.

According to one philosophy of life, it is the individual who personifies the highest value within our world. A physician, being an ethical individualist, will find himself harassed by conflicting duties. Sympathy for his patient will warn him against revealing the truth; his moral conviction will urge him to divulge it.

According to a different philosophy of life, the community personifies the highest value. The physician, for example, has reason to assume that the patient, if he knew the truth, would dispose of his fortune in favor of a charitable institution or a research project. The interest of the public in seeing the patient's intention carried out would morally oblige the physician to tell the patient the truth concerning his disease. Or, suppose a political leader intends to write a political will containing directions as to foreign affairs. The physician, should he know of this intention, certainly would feel obliged to urge him to do so before it is too late.

It is obvious that ethics and morals cannot lead to a

single valid answer. Yet, as we have shown, the unique relation between the physician and his patient may create a responsibility which no longer is a matter of medical skill. Legal maxims, conceived by the Romans and ever since adapted to the changing conditions of life, may yield a workable solution.

The law decrees discretion for a group of professionals to whom the physician belongs. It also recognizes the duty of these professionals to reveal the knowledge they acquired by practicing their profession if there are "predominant public or private interests." The interest of the patient that secrecy be observed is then of minor importance; the breach of confidence is legally justified. The physician's action is a "protection of legitimate rights." The illustrations used before, such as the notification of the Board of Health or the warning given to the betrothed, are examples. By communicating his knowledge to the people concerned, the physician tries to obviate a damage which otherwise probably would occur. He is legally bound to do so.

Our problem here differs in so far from the cases cited above, as the patient himself is the one to be informed. In relation to him, the physician is legally not obliged to observe secrecy. If he tells him the truth, a breach of confidence is out of the question. Nevertheless, the rule which justifies such breach in case where the physician reveals the nature of his patient's disease to another person, namely "the protection of legitimate rights," offers a workable solution by conclusion from analogy.

The intention of the patient to dispose of his fortune (or part of it) for a charitable purpose or in favor of a scientific project creates, as we have seen, a predominant interest of the public in having this intention carried out.

The same may hold true in regard to a private person, let us say, a gifted nephew of the patient, whose education the patient wants to secure by bequeathing to him a certain sum. The assumption seems justified that the patient himself, if informed of the truth, will feel that carrying out his intention is more important than the peace of his mind. His own interest will coincide with that of the public or another private person. Thus, if both parties have the same predominant interest, the mere possibility that the patient might feel uneasy when knowing the truth is of minor importance. We arrive at the conclusion that the physician is legally obliged to tell his patient the truth, if this is necessary to secure the materialization of a predominant interest of another person (the public or a private person) and of the patient himself.

Up to this time, legal authorities have not been induced to advance their opinion regarding our problem, and one should not expect to find our conclusion confirmed by statutes or jurisdiction. Rather, it is meant to serve as a guide in the event that some day wider circles will be preoccupied with it and the courts or even the legislature will be called upon to solve it.

A Lawyer's Advice

By William F. Martin

Our question is when and under what circumstances a fatally ill patient should be told the prognosis of his condition. The presence of incurable cancer is a classic example. In my experience for many years as counsel for the New York State Medical Society I have seen no decision or any legislation that attempts to invade the field of the doctor's prerogative and lay down a definite rule that is applicable to this situation.

No case has become known to me in which a physician was sued or could have been sued for failing to tell a seriously ill patient the truth about his disease. Financial complications arising from the lack of such orientation have never been the basis of legal procedings against the physician.

Similarly, I do not know of any case in which a physician was sued because he told the patient the truth, with the result that the patient attempted or committed suicide. I do not believe that the physician is legally responsible in any manner.

There have been actions brought because *no member of the family* was told that the doctor thought the patient had cancer; and there have been lawsuits against doctors who thought they removed the cancer but did not tell the family that it was a cancer so that the family could thereafter be on the alert as to what the patient should be prepared for. This situation would seem to make it necessary that a member of the family be told the truth whenever the operation discloses cancer; it might also create the necessity for alerting a patient without a family to keep in touch with the doctor because the patient's condition may recur and even lead to death if it is not properly watched.

Acknowledgements

For arrangements made with various publishing houses, authors, and literary agents whereby certain copyrighted material was permitted to be reprinted, and for the courtesy extended by them, acknowledgements are gratefully made. Full bibliographic data will be found in the chapters containing the reprinted material.

To Dr. Owen H. Wangensteen and the C. V. Mosby Company for the use of his June, 1950, editorial in Surgery which we are including here in slightly modified form.

To Dr. E. M. Bluestone and The Modern Hospital for letting us reprint the portions of an extensive paper that relate directly to the subject of our book.

To Dr. Bernard C. Meyer and The Journal of the Mount Sinai Hospital for his paper "Should The Patient Know The Truth?"

To the New England Journal of Medicine for the portions taken from Dr. H. J. Henderson's "Physician and Patient as a Social System."

To Mrs. Hans Zinsser for quotations from her late husband's autobiographical novel, "As I Remember Him."

To Mrs. Edith Rosenzweig and the Schocken Verlag for a passage from Franz Rosenzweig's "Briefe."

ACKNOWLEDGEMENTS

To the Noonday Press (Schocken Books, Inc.) for two further passages by Rosenzweig which were taken from his "Life and Thought" presented by N. N. Glatzer.

To the Newman Press for the quotation from F. J. Connell's "Morals in Politics and Professions."

To the Catholic Hospital Association for quotations from its "Ethical and Religious Directives for Catholic Hospitals," and from G. Kelly's "Should the Cancer Patient be Told?"

To the John Hopkins Press for two passages taken from "The Jews and Medicine" by Harry Friedenwald.

To the Hebrew Publishing Company for several passages taken from "Kitzur Shulhan Arukh."

To Paul B. Hoeber, Inc., for the words from W. L. Sperry's "The Ethical Basis of Medical Practice."

To Henry Holt and Company for permitting quotation of Robert Frost's short poem "Bravado" and for the lines taken from his poem "Home Burial."

To Brandt and Brandt and Rinehart & Company, Inc. for the sentences from "No Visitors" by Stephen Vincent Benet.

This book was set by THE POLYGLOT PRESS and printed at THE PROFILE PRESS, New York.